After Race

After Race

Racism after Multiculturalism

Antonia Darder and
Rodolfo D. Torres

NEW YORK UNIVERSITY PRESS

New York and London

NEW YORK UNIVERSITY PRESS
New York and London
www.nyupress.org

Library of Congress Cataloging-in-Publication Data
Darder, Antonia.
After race : racism after multiculturalism /
Antonia Darder and Rodolfo D. Torres.
p. cm.
Includes bibliographical references and index.
ISBN 0–8147–8268–X (cloth : alk. paper) —
ISBN 0–8147–8269–8 (pbk. : alk. paper)
1. Race—Social aspects.   2. Racism.   3. Marginality, Social.
4. Racism—United States.   5. Minorities—United States.
6. United States—Race relations.   I. Torres, Rodolfo D., 1949–
II. Title.
HT1521.D37   2004
305.8'0973—dc22   2004005810

New York University Press books are printed on acid-free paper,
and their binding materials are chosen for strength and durability.

Manufactured in the United States of America

c 10 9 8 7 6 5 4 3 2 1
p 10 9 8 7 6 5 4 3 2 1

We dedicate this book to our mothers,
Mary Najera and Carmen Francisca Aguilo Rosario,
whose lives of suffering and poverty fueled our impetus
to struggle—though their stories could never illuminate
the complex truth of the savage structures of inequality
that ruled our lives on the streets of East Los Angeles.
For this, we turned to Marx.

Contents

Acknowledgments

We wish to express our appreciation to our colleagues and students for the insights and support they have offered us in the development of our work. In particular, we thank Robert Miles for his friendship and mentorship, as well as his contributions to the intellectual tradition he has worked to forge during these perilous times. Mil gracias to Mario Barrera, Victor Valle, Maulana Karenga, John Solomos, Kevin Johnson, Lou Mirón, Suzanne Oboler, and David Roediger for their thoughtful and challenging responses to our ideas, as well as to Satnam Virdee for his cross-Atlantic input to this work. None of these fine individuals are to be held responsible for our errors and failures. In fact, several of our colleagues have expressed disagreement with our theoretical arguments, but, nevertheless, they agree on the need for this political and intellectual intervention. We remain open to continued conversations on this timely and important topic. A very special thanks to Nancy Christensen, Laura Galicia, and Joseph Feria-Galicia for their invaluable assistance in the preparation of this manuscript. And last, we thank our families for their patience and support through all the ups and downs of living with our creative angst.

After Race

An Introduction

The truth is that there are no races. . . . The evil that is done is done
by the concept and by—yet impossible—assumptions as to its application. What we miss through our obsession . . . is, simply, reality.
(Appiah 1995, 75)

Over a century ago, W. E. B. Du Bois in *The Souls of Black
Folk* proclaimed one of his most cited dictums: "The problem of the 20th
Century is the problem of the color line" (1989, 10). In this book we echo
his sentiment, but with a radical twist. The problem of the twenty-first
century is the problem of "race"—an ideology that has served well to successfully obscure and disguise class interests behind the smokescreen of
multiculturalism, diversity, difference, and more recently, whiteness.
Whether the terms of analysis are "race," "racial identity," "race consciousness," or "political race," the category of "race" and its many de-
rivatives function as the lynchpin of racism, which "forbids its objects to
be other than members of a race" (Fields 2001, 49). As Barbara Fields has
noted with respect to African Americans,

Afro-Americans themselves have fought successively for different ways
of naming themselves as people. . . . Each name, once accepted into the
general public vocabulary, has simply become a variant word for Afro-
Americans' race. A sense of peoplehood, nationhood, or comradeship in
struggle may be available to others; but, for persons of African descent,
all reduces to race, a life sentence for them and their issue in perpetuity.
(50)

1

To radically shift directions and speak "against race," as Paul Gilroy (2000) suggests, or "after race" as we attempt to do here, is to uncompromisingly refuse to accept or legitimate any longer the perpetual racialized demarcations of "raced" (Guinier and Torres 2002) or "problem" (Du Bois 1989) populations. Our intention is to contest the notion that the color of a person's skin, and all it has historically come to signify within the sociological, political, or popular imagination, should continue to function as such. We seek to shatter dubious claims that essentialize the responses of populations, whether they exist as objects or subjects of racism; and by so doing, acknowledge the complexity of the world in which we negotiate our daily existence today.

To be clear, we are not arguing in the tradition of the color-blind conservatives or political pundits who would have us believe that the structures and practices that have formidably embedded racism as a way of life for centuries in the United States and around the world have been undone and that the problem of racism has been ameliorated. Our position, in fact, is diametrically opposed to this argument. Instead, the political force of our analysis is anchored in the centrality of "race" as an ideology and racism as a powerful, structuring, hegemonic force in the world today. We argue that we must disconnect from "race" as it has been constructed in the past, and contend fully with the impact of "race" as ideology on the lives of all people—but most importantly on the lives of those who have been enslaved, colonized, or marked for genocide in the course of world history.

Situating the Debate

We have arrived at this position after ten long years of debate and research into the extremely murky, contradictory, and disturbing literature in the field. During this time, a variety of questions have informed our work, questions that the reader will find repeatedly reflected or inferred in the collection of interpretive essays included in this book. Some of these questions include: How has the notion of "race" changed over time? What analytical value or utility does the concept of "race" have in our struggle against racism and economic inequality? What value do contemporary notions of "race" have in our efforts to dismantle the external material structures of oppression that sustain racialized inequalities? Should we jettison the concept of "race" but continue to study racism?

Can racism exist without "races"? Does the concept of "race" have any real referent in the social world beyond its link to racism as an ideology? What is the relationship between changing class formations and racialized inequalities? What are the problematics of "white supremacy" arguments in the antiracist struggle for economic democracy? To what extent do retaining black-white dichotomous perceptions of "race relations" render other racialized populations invisible? Is the black-white paradigm of "race relations" able to grasp the new patterns of conflict or racialized inequalities within a changing political economy? What are the implications of questioning the "race relations" paradigm? How can we arrive at a more precise and specific concept with which to analyze both the historical and contemporary social realities and material conditions of racialized inequalities? What new strategies might help us dissolve the historical barriers that interfere with the establishment of antiracism solidarity across populations with quite different histories of integration into the U.S. body politic?

The posing of these difficult questions should not be interpreted to mean that white-on-black racism is not a significant and necessary area of study. Rather, we believe that breaking with the black-white racism problematic can open up new research possibilities in comparative studies of racialized inequalities that could potentially reinvigorate our political efforts to ameliorate human suffering. As we attempt to address different aspects of these questions in this book, we want to state explicitly that our critique of the race problematic goes beyond positing that biological "races" do not exist or the claim that the concept of "race" is socially and culturally constructed. Despite the proverbial caveat of "social construction," the analytical and descriptive (or discursive) categories of "race" lead to some serious theoretical problems, as we suggest in the following chapters. Thus, we contend that the everyday use of "race" for symbolic or political purposes must be uprooted, along with outdated biological assertions. In so doing, our attention will be focused on how best to conceptualize multiple racisms and racialized formations within the context of demographic shifts, changing capitalist class relations, and global socioeconomic dislocations.

The debate over such questions is not new. European and Australian, as well as American social scientists such as Collette Guillaumin, Robert Miles, Paul Gilroy, Stuart Hall, Kenan Malik, Etienne Balibar, Michael Omi, Howard Winant, Stephen Castles, David Theo Goldberg, Stephen Small, Anthony Appiah, William Julius Wilson, Barbara Fields, and others have been examining questions such as these since the 1980s. Most notable among them is Robert Miles, a British sociologist, who in 1982 first blew open the debate on the analytical utility of "race" as a suitable construct for the sociological analysis of human populations. Miles called into question the "race relations" paradigm that had dominated the field since the 1960s. Importantly, his efforts have assisted Marxist scholars in recovering class analysis as a significant analytical tool in the examination of racism at a time when postmodern theories began to severely curtail and erode the analytical power of this approach in scholarly examinations of culture. In addition, Miles has pointed to the need for scholars to engage the historical specificity, rather than to adhere to a view of singularity, in theorizing racism. He has argued that historically specific racisms possess their own "effectivity" and as such, could operate as a constitutive (determinant) force in shaping the ideology of the time. Two decades later, this critique remains compelling and instructive but conspicuously missing as we navigate through the contemporary debate.

Along with the writings in the study of "race" and racism, the work of Ellen Meiksins Wood has been significant to our understanding of contemporary capitalism (with its unrelenting project of modernization) and its impact on the de-democratization of public life within nation-states. Wood's (1995) efforts to rethink democracy without capitalism constitute a powerful treatise that unapologetically points to capitalism as the most engulfing system of social relations in the history of humankind. Wood insists that we recognize power as unrelentingly anchored in external material conditions and remain ever cognizant of the social impact of the mode of production upon workers, in this country and abroad. That is, we cannot ignore the increasing significance of class and the specificity of capitalism as a system of social and political relations of power, particularly in light of current struggles to contend with the virulent particularities of globalized racisms. The failure to engage the political economy and its impact on class formations—inherent in all contemporary expressions of racism—is a severe shortcoming in many of the scholarly treatments of "race" during the last fifty years. Moreover, we need greater specificity in the language we use to talk about the complexities of class, the economy, and social power in contemporary formations of racialized inequalities.

The Idea of "Race"

The research on contemporary racism points to an arresting dilemma. Social scientists seem befuddled in their efforts to extend their analysis beyond the traditional "racial" classifications sustained by the idea of "race." This can be briefly articulated in the following manner. "Race" has no scientific basis, yet racial categorization certainly foregrounds social structure and action. The majority of people in this country continue to believe that they belong to a specific race, and this has an impact on the way they conceive of their social identity. Hence, it can be said that for many racism functions to define both Self and Other. This is apparent in racialized discourses of hierarchy, in which members of dominant groups assert their superiority over other groups, and in racialized discourses of solidarity, in which subordinated groups assert their unity and rights. As such, "race may not be a biological fact, but it certainly is a social reality" (Castles 1996, 22)—a social reality kept alive by the relentless use of "race" to construct meaning within both academic and popular culture.

The history of "race" as ideology is equally puzzling. In early writings, categories used to define people were both similar to and different from the way we conceptualize "race" today. For example, it was not unusual for English writers to refer to the Irish as an inferior "race." However, their judgments were not necessarily linked to biological determinism but rather to cultural or social determinants, such as nationality or religion. It was not until the legacy of Darwin seeped into the popular imagination that the belief in "race" as a genetic predisposition of social behavior flourished. The concept of "race" has always been linked to either social or genetic constructions of inferiority or superiority assigned to particular populations, depending on the term's historical usage and reference. The ideology of "race" and its use, whether as a construct in the interest of genocide and colonialism or in the interest of political resistance, has always engendered the seeds of essentialism. So, if "race" is "real," it is only "because we have acted as if certain people, at certain points in time, were inferior based on innate or essentialized characteristics" (Lee, Mountain, and Koenig 2001, 40). Hence, the circularity of "race" logic leaves little possibility outside the realm of determinism. The power that ratifies "race" thinking is, wittingly or unwittingly, grounded in the notion that "race," whether biological or cultural, is immutable—indivisible from the essential character of individuals.

Although today "race" is generally linked to phenotypic characteristics, there is a strong consensus among evolutionary biologists and genetic anthropologists that "biologically identifiable human races do not exist; *Homo sapiens* constitute a single species, and have been so since their evolution in Africa and throughout their migration around the world" (Lee, Mountain, and Koenig 2001, 39). This perspective is similar to that which existed prior to the eighteenth century, when the notion that there were distinct populations whose differences were grounded in biology did not exist. For the Greeks, for example, the term "barbarian" was tied to how civilized a people were considered to be (generally based on language rather than genetics). So how did all this begin?

George Fredrickson (2002), writing on the history of racism, identifies the anticipatory moment of modern racism with the "treatment of Jewish converts to Christianity in fifteenth- and sixteenth-century Spain. *Conversos* were identified and discriminated against because of the belief held by Christians that the impurity of their blood made them incapable of experiencing a true conversion" (31). Fredrickson argues that the racism inherent in the quasi-religious, Spanish doctrine of *limpeza de sangre,* referring to purity of blood, set the stage for the spread of racism to the New World:

> To the extent that it was enforced represented the stigmatization of an entire ethnic group on the basis of deficiencies that allegedly could not be eradicated by conversion or assimilation. Inherited social status was nothing new; the concept of "noble blood" had long meant that the offspring of certain families were born with a claim to high status. But when the status of large numbers of people was depressed purely and simply because of their derivation from a denigrated *ethnos*, a line had been crossed that gave "race" a new and more comprehensive significance. (33)

Hence, religious notions, steeped in an ideology of "race," played a significant role in the exportation of racism into the Americas, where domination by the superior "race" was perceived as "inevitable and desirable, because it was thought to lead to human progress" (Castles 1996, 21).

The emergence of "race" as ideology can also be traced to the rise of nationalism. Efforts by nation-states to extend or deny rights of citizenship contingent on "race" or "ethnicity" were not uncommon, even within so-called democratic republics. Here, national mythology about those with "the biological unfitness for full citizenship" (Fredrickson 2002, 68) served to sanction exclusionary practices, despite the fact that all people shared "the historical process of migration and intermingling" (Castles 1996, 21). Herein is contained the logic behind what Valle and Torres (2000) term "the policing of race," a condition that results in official policies and practices by the nation-state designed to exclude or curtail the rights of racialized populations. In Germany, the Nazi regime took the logic of "race" to its pinnacle, rendering Jewish and Gypsy populations a threat to the state, thus rationalizing and justifying their demise. This example disrupts the notion that racism occurs only within the context of black-white relations. Instead, Castles (1996) argues that economic exploitation has always been central to the emergence of racism. Whether it incorporated slavery or indentured servitude, racialized systems of labor were perpetrated in Europe against immigrants, including Irish, Jewish, and Polish workers, as well as against indigenous populations around the world.

In the midst of the "scientific" penchant of the eighteenth century, Carolus Linneaus developed one of the first topologies to actually categorize human beings into four distinct subspecies: *americanus, asiaticus, africanus,* and *europeaeus.* Linneaus's classification, allegedly neutral and scientific, included not only physical features but also behavioral characteristics, hierarchically arranged in accordance with the prevailing social values and the political-economic interests of the times. The predictable result is the current ideological configuration of "race" used to both explain and control social behavior.

Etienne Balibar's (2003) work on racism is useful in understanding the ideological justifications that historically have accompanied the exclusion and domination of racialized populations—a phenomenon heavily fueled by the tensions of internal migration in the current era of globalization.

> [R]acism describes in an abstract idealizing manner "types of humanity," and . . . makes extensive use of classifications which allow all individuals and groups to imagine answers for the most immediate existential questions, such as imposition of identities and the permanence of violence between nations, ethnic or religious communities. (3)

Balibar also points to the impact of "symbolic projections and media-tions" (in particular, stereotypes and prejudices linked to divine-human-ity or bestial-animality) in the construction of racialized formations. "Racial" classification becomes associated with a distinction between the "properly human" and its imaginary (animal-like) "other." Such projec-tions and mediations, Balibar argues, are inscribed with modernity's ex-pansionist rationality—a quasi-humanist conception that suggests that differences and inequalities are the result of unequal access and social ex-clusion from cultural, political, or intellectual life but also implies that these differences and inequalities represent normal patterns, given the level of "humanity" or "animality" attributed to particular populations. James Baldwin in "A Talk to Teachers" (1988) links this phenomenon of racialization to the political economy and its impact on African Ameri-cans.

> The point of all this is that Black men were brought here as a source of cheap labor. They were indispensable to the economy. In order to justify the fact that men were treated as though they were animals, the white re-public had to brain wash itself into believing that they were indeed ani-mals and deserved to be treated like animals. (7)

Lee, Mountain, and Koenig (2001) note, "the taxonomy of race has al-ways been and continues to be primarily political" (43). Since politics and economics actually constitute one sphere, it is more precise to say that the ideology of "race" continues to be primarily about political economy. Thus, historians of "race" and racism argue that the idea of immutable, biologically determined "races" is a direct outcome of exploration and colonialism, which furnished the "scientific" justification for the eco-nomic exploitation, slavery, and even genocide of those groups perceived as subhuman.

Racialized Constructions

The veiled history of racialized taxonomy continues to be at work today, under the auspices of the national census system. Since its inception in 1790, the U.S. Census Bureau has gathered information on "race." Cri-teria utilized over the years have included nationality, tribal affiliation, as well as indicators of "blood" (i.e., mulatto, quadroon, octoroon). This eventually resulted in the current framework mandated by the U.S. Office of Management and Budget (OMB)—a framework inspired by an ideology of "race."

> [This] framework of identifying race focused on lineage and implicitly defined "whiteness" by a standard of genetic "purity," despite physiological markers that may give the appearance of whiteness or blackness. This rule, although no longer embraced officially by the government, reflects a belief in the biological basis for group differences that continues to characterize racial thinking in the United States. (Lee, Mountain, and Koenig 2001, 43)

In the twentieth century, the U.S. Census Bureau utilized twenty-six distinct classification designs for measuring "race." By the year 2000, all non-European groups had been collapsed into four (nonwhite) categories and two ethnicities, including the category "some other race." In a separate question, all respondents were also asked to identify their "ethnicity." As has been documented by the research related to the 2000 census, respondents often experienced confusion in distinguishing between "race" and ethnicity.

Stephen Castles (1996) argues, "racism chooses its targets according to its own perverse inner logic, rather than on the basis of some fixed hierarchical taxonomy" (28). In response to this inner logic, the state continues to preserve a vested interest in the control and management of diverse populations. Through its power to legislate "race relations"—the social relations between people of different "races"—the reality of "race" is legitimated by law (Guillaumin 1980). To illustrate this point, Manning Marable (2000) cites the emergence of the term "Hispanic":

> The U.S. government's decision in 1971 to create a new "ethnic," but not "racial," category of "Hispanic" on its census form is the best recent example of state manipulation of the politics of difference. The designation of "Hispanic" was imposed on more than fifteen million citizens and resident aliens who had very different nationalities, racial-ethnic identities, cultures, social organizations, and political histories. (B4)

Such machinations by the state to regulate "identities" both fuel and ignite a foundational belief in the unexamined assumption that "race" (or ethnicity) equals "identity." Consequently, the strangest political bedfellows result—white right-wing conservatives in bed with black or Chicano nationalists in bed with Latino politicos—all of whom would readily refute any perspective that sought to eliminate "race" as an explanatory category of analysis. Gilroy (2000) argues that for those mired in the immutable belief in "race" as identity, "the idea that priceless, essential identities are in perpetual danger from the difference outside them and that their precious purity is always at risk from the impressible power of heteroculture has certainly supplied the pivot for some unlikely political alliances" (221). The results of such alliances have been well evidenced, for instance, in educational struggles related to standardized testing and charter school initiatives or public policy debates concerning welfare rights, abortion rights, gun control, or gay and lesbian civil rights.

"Race" today continues to exist as part of a commonsense discourse that encompasses the accumulated and often contradictory assumptions used by people to decipher and contend with the complex world around us. This is why the influence of past ideologies and practices makes itself known and felt, directly and indirectly, through the racialized discourse of the media, political officials, and popular culture, even in ostensibly democratic societies. For recent examples, we need only recall the racialized discourse of the Bush administration to justify military action against Afghanistan and Iraq, economic blockades in Venezuela, and threats with weapons of mass destruction against North Korea. From the halls of Congress, we need only summon reports on the segregationist assertions of former majority whip Trent Lott and the racialized justifications of Howard Coble for the use of severe "security" measures to "protect" Japanese citizens during World War II. And even on the pages of *Vanity Fair* (February 2003), Dame Edna (pseudonym for Barry Humphries) is given license, in the spirit of satirical humor, to express racialized wisdom. To "Torn Romantic from Palm Beach," who is agonizing over whether to learn Spanish or French, Dame Edna responds:

> Forget Spanish. There's nothing in that language worth reading except Don Quixote, and a quick listen to the CD of Man of La Mancha will take care of that. There was a poet named Garcia Lorca, but I'd leave him on the intellectual back burner if I were you. As for everyone's speaking it, what twaddle! Who speaks it that you are really desperate to talk to? The help? Your leaf blower? Study French or German, where

there are at least a few books worth reading, or, if you're American, try English.

These examples illustrate how the power of racialized discourse "allows elite groups to claim enlightened and meritocratic views, while applying racist definitions of social reality" (Castles 1996, 30). Such forms of racialized discourse effectively perpetuate what Miles (1989) terms racialization—an ideological process of "delineation of group boundaries and of allocation of persons within those boundaries by primary reference to (supposedly) inherent and/or biological (usually phenotypical) characteristics" (74). The use of racialization here encompasses a "dialectical process of signification where those characteristics that are ascribed to define the Other, necessarily elicit a definition of the Self by the same criterion" (75).[1]

It is the process of racialization, with its reified commonsense notions of "race," that sustains the study of "race relations," an approach that has dominated the field for almost half a century. As a consequence of the "race relations" paradigm, U.S. society became further entrenched in the language of "race" as destiny, with an implicit dictum that membership in particular "races" enacted social processes rather than ideology. This approach has effectively fueled the racialization of politics, through which political discourses of many kinds are structured by attaching deterministic meaning to social constructs of physical and cultural characteristics. The outcome is the racialization of all social and political relations, infusing every conflict of interest with an ethnic dimension, so that racism becomes a way of expressing group interests (Ball and Solomos 1990). Fields (2001), an acerbic critic of "race relations," describes its impact on the engagement of the "Negro problem."

> The ideological formation of race relations skirted the considerable difficulty of stating the Negro problem within the forms of a purportedly democratic polity and with respect to persons who were nominally citizens in that polity enjoying full political rights. Race relations so suited the liberal thought of the time, and has been so well able to accommodate the internal twists of liberal and neo-liberal thought since, that it remains a vital part of the prevailing public language today. It lingers on to cozen scholars who, instead of investigating it as an ideological device, accept it ingenuously as an empirical datum. (54)

While we argue against attributing explanatory or descriptive value to "race," we do not mean to suggest that races have no social reality—they do. This fiction of "race" is produced in the real world, thus serving to legitimate it and give it conceptual meaning and social life. At its core, the effort to transmute the concept of "race" into an objective reality is limited and, as Appiah (cited in Postal 2002) concludes, a morally dangerous proposition. Hence, there is no need for a distinct (critical) theory of "race"; instead, what is required is an earnest endeavor to theorize the specious concept with its illusory status out of existence and renew our commitment to the interrogation of racism as an ideology of social exclusion (Miles and Brown 2003).

In other words, if "race" is real, it is so only because it has been rendered meaningful by the actions and beliefs of the powerful, who retain the myth in order to protect their own political-economic interests. "Race" as a social construct of resistance comes into play only later, as racialized populations and their advocates embrace the concept in reverse to struggle against material conditions of domination and exploitation. Nevertheless, it cannot be denied that the essentialism inherent in the original epistemological intent of "race" is preserved. At its core, the effort to transmute the concept of "race" into an emancipatory category is a limited and unwise undertaking. Thus, it is high time we disrupt the continued use of a dubious concept that cannot help but render our theorizing ambiguous and problematic.

In its simplest terms, this ambiguity is most visible in the inconsistency with which the term "race" is applied—sometimes meaning ethnicity, at other times referring to culture or ancestry. More often than not, "terms used for race are seldom defined and race is frequently employed in a routine and uncritical manner to represent ill-defined social and cultural factors" (Williams 1994). This explains why in all the writings on "race" there is so little substantive theorizing about the construct itself. The category of "race" is thus suspect with respect to its analytical utility. If "race" is socially constructed and its origins clearly steeped in an ideology of exclusion, domination, exploitation, even genocide, why should we continue to make sense of people's lives based on the legacy of a pseudoscientific distortion from a previous era? Is not racism—as an ideology that exists within a structure of class differentiation and exploitation—rather than "race," the concept that merits our attention, particularly in these perilous times of global upheaval?

Theorizing Racism

Racism has been defined in a variety of ways, but certain points are central to our conceptualization of the term. First, racism is not the result of individual pathology; instead, it is an ideological set of practices and discourses embedded in the project of modernity and capitalist expansion. Second, racism is linked to racialization, a process by which populations are categorized and ranked on the basis of phenotypical traits or cultural signifiers. Economic and political power is implicated because of its explicit (or implicit) purpose of legitimating the exploitation or exclusion of racialized groups. And third, there is no one generic form, but rather multiple, diverse, and historically specific racisms that may vary in intensity, but constitute part and parcel of the larger phenomenon (Goldberg 1993; Castles 1996).

Etienne Balibar and Immanuel Wallerstein (1991) argue that in order to make our studies of racism more specific we must distinguish between two forms of racism. The first refers to those racisms whose primary intent is the exclusion and extermination of racialized populations deemed a threat. The second, termed *"inferiorization,"* is found in modern situations of migrant labor where labor rights are denied, forcing immigrant workers to take menial jobs and low entry positions that all others are unwilling to accept. Generally speaking, these two forms of racism "exist side by side and are linked to class interests. The ruling class is more likely to be interested in the racism of exploitation, while workers may favor exclusion" (Castles 1996, 26). This should come as no surprise, given that economic and political relations have been constructed in concert with the ideology of racism.

The reduction of racism to white racism against nonwhites is usually linked to post-1945 anticolonial and civil rights movements. However, Miles (1989) traces the roots of this process to early colonial life.

[T]here is a universal dimension to [the] process of spatial segregation in so far as every ruling class usually organises its life in a distinct spatial location, separated from the lives of those whose labour power is exploited. The specificity lies in the conscious and strategic institutionalisation of a particular representational construction, that is, racism. The ideology of racism was used to not only select certain people to fill certain positions in the structure of class relations but class relations were themselves structured in a particular manner to create a large proportion of Africans as suppliers of cheap labour. (111)

This explanation sheds light on the evolution of racism against ethnic minority workers in Europe and against indigenous populations in Latin America, Africa, and Asia. The multiplicity of racisms currently expressed on the international stage in the face of globalization counters singular black-white notions of racism, so prevalent in the United States. Within U.S. cities, changing demographic profiles associated with a rapidly increasing immigrant population also expose the limits of a black-white paradigm. In its place, more complex configurations of racialized populations are evolving, as "the phenotypical, color-based categories of differences that only a generation ago appeared rigid and fixed are being restructured and reconfigured against the background of globalized capitalism and neo-liberal government policies worldwide" (Marable 2000, 9). But such change is slow and uneven; and newly arrived immigrants often find themselves confusingly initiated into the rigidity of black-white racialized relations. Nevertheless, Fields (2001) argues that

the real issue is not how immigrants became white or black, but how persons not born and bred to it, whatever their ancestry, become oriented in the American world of black and white. When the dichotomy was not completely irrelevant in the immigrants' place of origin (as for most European immigrants), it would have been overlaid with other pairs—peasant/landlord, villager/chief, native/colonial, illiterate/educated, inigene/evolue, black/brown (or coloured)—that fundamentally distinguished it from the stark opposition that prevailed in the United States. (52)

Given the complexity of our times, Castles (1996) rightly suggests that any study of racism requires an interdisciplinary approach in order to arrive at a more precise understanding of the different economic, political, and cultural factors which engender its existence. Theories of racism must be sufficiently comprehensive as to take into account the great diversity among and between populations "without losing sight of their essential unity" (20), anchored in the fact that we are all human beings belonging to one species that descended from Africa. Hence, we must develop theories that can negotiate both the commonality and plurality of racisms, anchored, as Goldberg (1993) suggests, in the "historical alterations and discontinuities" (41) that give rise to their ideological formations and their explicit social practices. Theories of racism must also grapple with the development of strategies and counterpractices for dismantling the hegemonic structures that give rise to its consequences.

As we have suggested, scholars have tended to study "race" rather than racism. New scholarly texts on "race" are released daily, particularly in England, Australia, and the United States. Everywhere scholars seem eager to address "race" with its myriad of racial identities—including whiteness. Indeed, even the media has discovered the currency of "race." For example, on September 18, 2000, *Newsweek* published a special report entitled "Redefining Race in America." On the cover was a photographic collage of a variety of dismembered phenotypic representations, including hair, eyes, lips, and skin color. One of the feature stories, "The New Faces of Race," included a variety of photographs depicting "a gallery of native-born Americans." All those depicted were captioned with no less than three (racial, ethnic, national) labels to connote racial identities. In the text, reference was made to thirty census categories—a scheme that, as suggested earlier, is far more attached to the racialized constructions of the ivory tower and government officials than to what is actually taking place on the streets. Consequently, official labels obscure rather than illuminate the social and political experiences and realities of racialized populations in the United States (Oboler 1995).

This then begs the question as to why so many scholars (and politicians) are willing to speak of "race" as a reified, commonsense category of analysis in the construction of social theories and the development of public policy. Why do class analysis or challenges to capitalism—an overarching material force linked to the survival (or destruction) of people worldwide—not receive the level of treatment and regard accorded to the study of "race"? In today's virtual reality where capital transits the globe at lightning speed, there seems to be little tolerance for serious scholarly or political interrogations of capitalism as an ideology of modernity run amuck. Even many scholars of multiculturalism who solemnly proclaim that the purpose of their work is social justice have failed to critically examine capitalism.

Forthright analyses of racism, as not only one of the most effective hegemonic forces of our time in sustaining the interests of capitalist exploitation and domination but also as the progenitor of one of the greatest fallacies of history—the idea that "races" truly exist—are few and far between. Could it be that scholars worldwide find themselves so deeply entrenched or implicated that close analysis would find us all mired in contradiction, while supporting the very system responsible for so much human suffering in the first place? In response, Fields (2001) contrasts the "homier and more tractable notion" of "race" with racism.

> Racism . . . unsettles fundamental instincts of American academic professionals who consider themselves liberal, leftist, or progressive. It is an act of peremptory, hostile, and supremely—often fatally—consequential identification that unceremoniously overrides its objects' sense of themselves. Racism thus unseats both identity and agency, if identity means sense of "self," and agency anything beyond conscious, goal directed activity, however trivial and ineffectual. The targets of racism do not "make" racism, nor are they free to "negotiate" the obstacles it places in their way. Even as racism exposes the hollowness of agency and identity, it violates the two-sides-to-every-story expectation of symmetry that Americans are peculiarly attached to. There is no voluntary and affirmative side to racism as far as its victims are concerned, and it has no respect for symmetry at all. That is why well-meaning scholars are more apt to speak of race than racism. (48)

This insight calls to mind the problematics of identity politics grounded in the simple and compelling premise that members of particular groups share a greater commonality than those considered outsiders. Although this may sometimes be the case, identity politics always hangs on the edge of essentialism, particularly when social (if not phenotypical) traits are generated as proof of both trustworthiness and political solidarity. Gilroy (2000) cautions against the myth of "short-cut solidarity" that such an approach engenders, particularly when identity and class are decoupled and the promise of identity politics falls flat on its face. Community interests easily become "diverted into middle class campaigns for affirmation, assimilation and 'a piece of the pie'" (Anner 1996, 9), while working-class and poor people see little improvement in the quality of their lives.

Moreover, when questions of identity and agency consistently displace questions of economic and social power, the structures of inequality are cleverly masked and it becomes difficult to change them. It is precisely this irreparable flaw of identity politics that drives Wood (1995) to challenge its validity. "The 'politics of identity' . . . purports to be both more fine-tuned in its sensitivity to the complexity of human experience and more inclusive in its emancipatory sweep than the old politics of socialism. . . . But the 'politics of identity' reveals its limitations, both theoretical and political, the moment we try to situate class differences within its democratic vision" (258).

Wood's critique allows us to segue to the methodological shortcomings of the intersectionality arguments, with its oft-repeated recitation of "race, class, and gender." While we agree with those who argue that racism, sexism, and class oppression are interrelated and intrinsic to modernity, we categorically disagree that a host of oppressions should be afforded equal analytical explanatory power while the unrivaled force of capitalism in the world today is ignored. Both racism and sexism are most certainly implicated in the hegemonic forces that result in class domination. However, it is the *material* domination and exploitation of populations, in the interest of perpetuating a deeply entrenched capitalist system of world dominion, which serves as the impetus for the construction of social formations of inequality. It is this reality that prompts Wood (1995) to ask: "Is it possible to imagine class difference without exploitation and domination?" Her response echoes our own critique of the intersectionality argument.

> The "difference" that constitutes class as an "identity" *is*, by definition, a relationship of inequality and power, in a way that sexual or cultural "difference" need not be. A truly democratic society can celebrate diversities of life styles, culture or sexual preference; but in what sense would it be "democratic" to celebrate class difference? If a conception of freedom or equality adapted to sexual and cultural differences is intended to extend the reach of human liberation, can the same be said of a conception of freedom or equality that accommodates *class* difference? (258; emphasis in original)

Such a critique of the intersectionality argument also raises concerns related to the manner in which scholars define the constitutive force of racism, an issue seldom addressed with any specificity in the literature on "race." So, are we to accept phylogenetic or socially constructed notions of "race" as eternal and, possibly, even as a precondition without which humankind could not evolve (Toynbee 1899 and Keith 1931, cited in Barot and Bird 2001)? Or should we see racism as a complex ideological apparatus of domination intricately linked to the conservation of power and control over resources and material wealth?

Relatedly, should we accept sexism as a pathology originating in the essentialized misogynist beliefs of men? Or is it a historical outgrowth of both patriarchal conquest and modernity, in the interest of dominance over material resources and the public institutions that govern their control? We are not arguing here against the notion that all forms of oppression are connected and act upon populations simultaneously. Instead, we argue that class, gender, sexuality, and racism do not have the same meaning or constitutive power—a highly significant issue for potentially reshaping political action in the coming years.

> At the very least, class equality means something different and requires different conditions from sexual or racial equality. In particular, the abolition of class inequality would by definition mean the end of capitalism. But is the same necessarily true about the abolition of sexual or racial inequality? Sexual and racial inequality . . . are not in principle incompatible with capitalism. The disappearance of class inequalities, on the other hand, is by definition incompatible with capitalism. At the same time, although class exploitation is constitutive of capitalism as sexual or racial inequality are not, capitalism subjects all social relations to its requirement. (Wood 1995, 259)

Racism and the Political Economy

Important to our understanding of racism, then, is the manner in which class and capitalism are inextricably linked in ways that do not apply to other categories of oppression. This perspective points to the social and political apparatus of the state that function systematically to retain widespread control and governance over material wealth and resources. This apparatus operates in conjunction with those ideologies (whether cultural, political, class, gendered, sexual, or racialized) that preserve the hegemony of the modern capitalist state, engendering its capacity to appropriate even revolutionary projects and strip them of their transformative potential.

Such has been the fate of multiculturalism which, falling prey to both the politics of identity and state appropriation, became an effective vehicle for further depoliticizing progressive efforts against inequality rooted in the civil rights era of the 1960s and 1970s. Notwithstanding its original emancipatory intent, the politics of multiculturalism was from its inception flawed by its adherence to the language of "race relations." Moreover, the well-meaning celebrations of difference and the hard-fought battles for representation by a variety of identity movements failed to generate any real or lasting structural change. Thus, liberal proposals such as affirmative action, for instance, more often than not served the interests of the more privileged. In the final analysis, multiculturalism became an effective mechanism of the state, used to manage and preserve racialized class divisions, while in the marketplace the new multiplicity of identities generated new products for consumption. Arun Kundnani (2002) describes the fate of multiculturalism in terms of black culture in England.

> Multiculturalism now meant taking black culture off the streets—where it has been politicised and turned into a rebellion against the state—and putting it in the council chamber, in the classroom and on the television, where it could be institutionalized, managed and reified. Black culture was thus turned from a living movement into an object of passive contemplation, something to be "celebrated" rather than acted on. Multiculturalism became an ideology of conservatism, of preserving the status quo intact, in the face of a real desire to move forward. As post-modern theories of "hybridity" became popular in academia, cultural difference came to be seen as an end in itself, rather than an expression of revolt, and the concept of culture became a straitjacket, hindering rather than helping the fight against [racism] and class oppressions. (2)

Large metropolitan areas across the United States have experienced similar events. Most notable in the 1990s was the aforementioned uprising in South Central Los Angeles, where the language of "race relations" coupled with a politics of difference dominated the discourse of the media. Sidestepped were the underlying class tensions, associated with the way in which "globalization, economic restructuring, and automation had transformed the Los Angeles industrial landscape" (Valle and Torres 2000, 61). Instead, the sensationalism of racialized images and "race relations" rhetoric prevailed for days, nonstop, on major television networks.

What was successfully camouflaged in Los Angeles was the fact that racism is not about cultural differences; it is about political economy. By converting racism into a conflict of cultural differences, whether it was between blacks and Latinos, or Latinos and Koreans, or blacks and whites, the commonsense notion of "race" was effectively preserved in Los Angeles and the inequality of class relations normalized. Thus people are socialized to perceive "race" as a matter of cultural (and often individual) differences, when in truth what generally passes under the guise of "race" are deeply entrenched racialized class relations. In the process, the political economy of racism, embedded in capitalism, effectively divides oppressed communities, leaving much of the world's population vulnerable to economic exploitation.

There are many who argue that the prevalent emphasis on cultural differences during the 1980s has brought with it a new wave of racism, unfettered by the old baggage of biological determinism. Balibar (1991), for instance, argues that this "new racism" is actually "racism without race" (23), an ideology that utilizes the covert belief in immutable human differences to assert the impossibility of coexistence. Meanwhile, class concerns are masked, while "the power of the dominant group to proclaim and manage hierarchies of acceptable and unacceptable difference" (Castles 1996, 29) shapes the rhetoric of community development, public policy debates, and global economic interests. In the same vein, Teun van Dijk (1993) argues that the dominance of the "new racism" on the global stage has remained unchanged. "This undeniable progress has only softened the style of dominance of . . . Western nations. Far from abolished are the deeply entrenched economic, social and cultural remnants of past oppression and inequality; the modern prejudices about minorities; the economic and military power or the cultural hegemony of white over black, north over south, majorities over minorities" (cited in Castles 1996, 30).

Undoubtedly, the globalization of the political economy, or rather the *universalization of capital* (Wood 1998), raises new and complex questions related to the changing nature of racism and class formations. However, we do not subscribe to the notion that the process of globalization reflects a grand epochal shift. As Wood argues, what we are seeing is not a major shift in the logic of capitalism but rather "the consequences of capitalism as a comprehensive system . . . capitalism reaching maturity" (47). Historically, then, globalization must be understood within the context of modernization—the process of European colonial expansionism since the fifteenth century. In his writings on the racisms of globalization, Castles (1996) links the Western project of modernity to racism:

Modernity implies increasingly integrated capitalist production and distribution systems, linked to secular cultures based on the principles of rationality. Modernity has meant colonization of the rest of the world, not only in the direct sense of political control, but also through diffusion of Western cultural values. Racism—as an ideology which justified European domination—has always been part of modernity. (19)

In agreement, we assert that the constitutive force of most contemporary racisms is closely aligned with labor transformations, systematically initiated by the economic expansionism of globalization. Castles (1996) provides a variety of examples to illustrate this point. These include: the oppression of indigenous peoples as legacies of colonialism; the decolonization and formation of new nation-states which frequently have resulted in the exploitation or exclusion of minority workers; violent struggles linked to the processes of globalization which have resulted in the movement of refugee populations within and outside their countries, resulting in the impoverishment and denial of human rights; the recruitment of migrant labor for the labor market, forcing wages down, with tensions ignited by the racialized conflict between native and immigrant workers; and the racism against old and new minorities which is contributing to the growing complexity of interethnic relations in urban centers and leading to new types of conflict and politicization, particularly on issues linked to culture and ethnicity.

Hence, the economic profiteering of transnational corporations, best illustrated by the Enron scandal,[2] has taken place on the backs of workers everywhere. Previously well-paying jobs in this country have been transferred to regions where cheap labor and little regulation enhances the profit margin of global enterprises. In cities such as Los Angeles, this phenomenon has given rise to high unemployment or underemployment, particularly among African American and Latino workers. The "global city" is now a place where jobs are few and immigration and poverty are high, while urban capital is heavily invested in complex international markets, eroding the political power of urban workers. Consequently, the cityscape continues to reflect previous segregation patterns of class and ethnicity, but in more complex and conflictual ways (Sassen 2001; Davis 1990; Valle and Torres 2000). In the large urban metropolis, the majority of the population is divested of any real opportunities for participation and decision-making, intensifying exclusionary practices. Yet, even in the midst of such entrenched inequalities, communities continue to seek out ways in which to launch antiracist struggles that might potentially impact the quality of their lives. Hence, we cannot ignore the myriad of popular movements that embrace antiracism as a key component of their organizing platform.

There is no question that to recognize racism as a central part of the social and political life of the capitalist state implies the need for radical change—change that would, undoubtedly, portend major shifts in the existing structures of inequality and asymmetrical relations of power. However, since the 1970s, antiracist advocates have blatantly ignored the centrality of class relations in the evolution and persistence of racism in U.S. society. Unwittingly, this neglect has led to the eruption of new racisms worldwide, as provincial attitudes prevailed. Absorbed with doing battle with what many deemed "economic determinism," antiracist advocates lost sight of the unfettered movement of capitalist interests around the globe as they attended to issues of identity and representation. Additionally, this approach prevented the formulation of a more substantive and comparative analysis of racism at the end of the twentieth century.

At this juncture, it seems important to say a few words regarding our approach to the study of racism, which we suspect will be characterized by some as privileging class or simply as economic determinism. If this is all that the reader gleans from our analysis, we certainly do not wish to debate the point; for we make no apologies for the centrality of our critique of capitalism and class formations in our analysis of racism. Furthermore, we have repeatedly stated, we do not argue against the notion that "race" is a social construction or that all relations of inequality merit examination. As such, our criticism of the black-white problematic is not intended to marginalize the study of white-on-black racism, but rather to recognize the existence of multiple modalities of racisms.

However, instead of falling in line with cultural studies or postmodern renditions of power, we concur with Joanne Naiman that we must rescue the concept of power from its diffused and unmeasurable position, everywhere and nowhere, back to where it holds the promise of collective political action. That is to say, where power is perceived as centered in the external, material world, rather than simply in people's heads. We firmly believe that this task is imperative to any political project that claims to counter racism in the world today. As Naiman (1996) argues,

> In any society where private property and social classes exist, those who own the means of production will dominate. This is most obvious in the

economic sphere, where those who own the productive units can decide what to produce, how to produce it, where to produce it, and so on. But the power of ownership goes far beyond mere economic control, and those who own the means of production also come to have power in the political and ideological spheres as well. Indeed, no owning class could maintain its position for long if it did not effectively control all three spheres within a society. (18)

Our work is in concert with those who seek to reclaim the power of working people—who, while less powerful than the owning class, are not powerless. The power of working-class people is embodied in the unequivocal fact that without their labor the capitalist class could not survive. In addition, workers are empowered through their sheer numbers. These are the qualities that along with important characteristics of organization make the working class central to our struggle against racism and social change. In our view, this has nothing to do with privileging class over other oppressions. Instead, it represents our evolving assessment of structural power, both actual and potential, of different groups within society—and the growing recognition that, no matter how one wishes to theorize "race" and racism, all forms of oppression are ultimately linked to the exploitation and domination of both natural resources and human populations.

As we continue to advance our arguments for a historical materialist approach to the study of racism, we find ourselves especially attentive to new political ideas and emancipatory visions that can advance the struggle for social justice, human rights, and economic democracy. One such possibility is the work currently being developed by U.S. scholars in the area of cultural citizenship. Cultural citizenship, initially advanced by Renato Rosaldo (1994), attempts to engage difficult and often conflicting questions of citizenship with respect to culture, identity, and political participation. Importantly, it seeks to understand differences significant to people along a continuum, in the hope of disrupting the racialized discourse of the "Other." As such, cultural citizenship as a political strategy seeks not only to establish a collectivity in which no one is left outside the system, but also to extend the rights of first-class citizenship to all people. Key to the concept is a critical universalism that fundamentally respects the particularities of populations while working to dismantle structures of inequality that interfere with the exercise of human rights. There is no doubt that many questions still remain to be answered, particularly about the manner in which cultural citizenship can "overcome the limitations of the state and embrace the body of human rights in the context of globalization, transnational movements, and localism" (Delgado-Moreira 1997, 2). But for the moment, it offers in its theoretical infancy a political promise—one that will need to forthrightly challenge capitalism and the ideology of "race" if it is to gain any currency within a world of overwhelming capital excesses and racialized inequalities.

In 1982, Robert Miles courageously did the unthinkable by challenging the utility of "race" in his efforts to construct an effective politics of antiracism. In 1996, Kenan Malik argued, in *The Meaning of Race,* that rather than embracing difference, we should strive to transcend "race" and embrace a human universality that contends with the particularities and differences of our existence. Paul Gilroy (2000) echoes both Miles and Malik, as he proposes a radical humanist project "against race" so that we may free ourselves of its bondage. Along with Miles, Gilroy, and Malik, we now call for a movement "after race," anchored in the radical proposition that we are not distinct "races" but rather, as Renato Rosaldo (1994) posits, cultural citizens—entitled to live in a world where economic, political, and cultural democracy is the birthright of all people, not the thievery of a few.

1

Does "Race" Matter?

Transatlantic Perspectives
on Racism after "Race Relations"

with Robert Miles

The survival of the United States as a democracy depends on the
dismantling of the race concept. (Graves 2001, 11)

In April 1993, one year after the Los Angeles civil unrest, a
major U.S. publisher published a book with the creatively ambiguous title
Race Matters by the distinguished scholar Cornel West. The back cover
of the slightly revised edition, published the following year, categorized it
as a contribution to both African American studies and current affairs.
The latter was confirmed by the publisher's strategy of marketing the
book as a "trade" rather than an "academic" title—this was a book for
the "American public" to read. And the American public was assured
that they were reading a quality product when they were told that its author had "built a reputation as one of the most eloquent voices in America's racial debate."

Some two years later, the *Los Angeles Times* (February 20, 1995) published an article by its science writer under the headline "Scientists Say
Race Has No Biological Basis." The opening paragraph ran as follows:

Researchers adept at analyzing the genetic threads of human diversity
said Sunday that the concept of race—the source of abiding cultural and
political divisions in American society—simply has no basis in fundamental human biology. Scientists should abandon it.

On the same day, the *Chronicle of Higher Education* reproduced the substance of these claims in an article entitled "A Growing Number of Scientists Reject the Concept of Race." Both publications were reporting on the proceedings of the American Association for the Advancement of Science in Atlanta. More recently, the December 2003 issue of *Scientific America* published an article entitled "Does Race Exist?" again challenging the notion of the existence of race and more importantly suggesting our human interconnections.

If the notion of "race" simply has no basis in fundamental human biology, how are we to evaluate West's assertion that "Race Matters"? If "race" matters, then surely "races" must exist! But if there are no "races," then "race" cannot matter. We do recognize that West employs the race concept as a symbolic and discursive term with no biological basis. But these two contributions to the public political debate of the 1990s seem to reveal a contradiction. Yet, within this arena of academic debate, a well-rehearsed attempt to dissolve the contradiction runs as follows. It is acknowledged that, earlier in the twentieth century, the biological and genetic sciences established conclusively in the light of empirical evidence that the attempt to establish the existence of different types or "races" of human beings by scientific procedures had failed. The idea that the human species consists of a number of distinct "races," each exhibiting a set of discrete physical and cultural characteristics, is therefore mistaken. The interventions reported as having been made in Atlanta in February 1995 only repeat what some scientists have been arguing since the 1930s. Yet, the fact that scientists have to continue to assert these claims demonstrates that the contrary is still widely believed and articulated in public discussion.

Because this scientific knowledge has not yet been comprehensively understood by "the general public" (which not only persists in believing in the existence of "races" as biologically discrete entities but also acts in ways consistent with such a belief), it is argued that social scientists must employ a *concept* of "race" to describe and analyze these beliefs and the discrimination and exclusion that are premised on this kind of classification. In other words, while social scientists know that there are no "races," they also know that things believed to exist (in this case "races") have a real existence for those who believe in them and that actions consistent with the belief have real social consequences. In sum, because people believe that "races" exist (i.e., because they utilize the *idea* of "race" to comprehend their social world), social scientists need a *concept* of "race."

Or do they? Preeminent amongst the reasons for such an assertion is that the arenas of academic and political discourse cannot be clinically separated. Hence West, in seeking to use his status as a leading Afro-American scholar to make a political intervention in current affairs by arguing that "Race Matters," is likely to legitimate and reinforce the widespread public belief that "races" exist, irrespective of his views on this issue. For if this belief in the existence of "races" were not widespread, there would be no news value in publishing an article in a leading daily U.S. newspaper that claims that "Race Has No Biological Basis."

Criticizing "Race" as an Analytical Category

We begin this exploration by crossing the Atlantic in order to consider the issue as it has been discussed in Britain for over 50 years. As we shall see, the development of the British discussion has, in fact, been influenced substantially by the preconceptions and language employed in the United States: the use of "race" as an analytical category in the social sciences is a transatlantic phenomenon.

It is now difficult to conceive, but in the 1950s no one would have suggested "Race Matters" *in Britain*. The idea of "race" was employed in public and political discussion largely in order to discuss "the colonies": the "race problem" was spatially located beyond British shores in the British Empire and especially in certain colonies, notably South Africa. This, too, had not always been so. During the nineteenth and early twentieth centuries, it was widely believed that the population of Britain was composed of a number of different "races" (for example, the Irish were identified as being "of the Celtic race"). Moreover, migration to Britain from central and eastern Europe in the late nineteenth century was interpreted by using the language of "race" to signify the Jewish refugees fleeing persecution (e.g., Barkan 1992, 15–65). But, as the situation in the port city of Liverpool after World War I suggested (e.g., Barkan 1992 57–65), the language of "race" used to refer to the interior of Britain was to be tied exclusively to differences in skin color in the second half of the twentieth century. What, then, was the "race" problem that existed beyond Britain's shores?

Briefly, the problem was perceived to be that the colonies were spatial sites where members of different "races" (Caucasian, white, African, Hindoo, Mongoloid, Celts: the language to name these supposed "races" varied enormously) met and where their "natures" (to civilize, to fight, to be lazy, to progress, to drink, to engage in sexual perversions, and so on) interacted, often with tragic consequences. This language of "race" was usually anchored in the signification of certain forms of somatic difference (skin color, facial characteristics, body shape and size, eye color, skull shape) which were interpreted as the physical marks which accompanied, and which in some unexplained way determined, the "nature" of those so marked. In this way, the social relations of British colonialism were explained as being "rooted" simultaneously in the biology of the human body and in the cultural attributes determined by "nature."

But the "race" problem was not to remain isolated from British shores, to be contained there by a combination of civilization and violence. All Her Majesty's subjects had the right of residence in the Motherland, and increasing numbers of them chose to exercise that right as the decade of the 1950s progressed. Members of the "colored races," from the Caribbean, and the Indian subcontinent in particular, migrated to Britain largely to fill vacancies in the labor market but against the will of successive governments (Labor and Conservative) who feared that they carried in their cheap suitcases not only their few clothes and personal possessions but also the "race problem" (e.g., Joshi and Carter 1984; Solomos 1989; Layton-Henry 1992). By the late 1950s, it was widely argued that, as a result of "colored immigration," Britain had imported a "race" problem. Prior to this migration, so it was believed, Britain's population was "racially homogeneous," a claim that neatly dispensed not only with earlier racialized classifications of both migrants and the population of the British Isles but also with the history of interior racisms (Miles 1993, 80–104).

The political and public response to immigration from the Caribbean and the Indian subcontinent is now a well-known story (e.g., Solomos 1989; Layton-Henry 1992), although there are a number of important byways still to be explored. What is of particular interest here is the academic response. A small number of social scientists (namely, sociologists and anthropologists) wrote about these migrations and their social consequences using the language of everyday life: *Dark Strangers* (Patterson 1963) and *The Colour Problem* (Richmond 1955) were the titles of two books that achieved a certain prominence during the late 1950s and early

1960s, and their authors subsequently pursued distinguished academic careers. Considered from the point of view of the 1990s, these titles now seem a little unfortunate and perhaps even a part of the problem insofar as they employ language that seems to echo and legitimate the racist discourse of the time.

But can the same be said for two other books that became classic texts within the social sciences: Michael Banton's *Race Relations* (1967) and John Rex's *Race Relations in Sociological Theory* (1970)? Both were published in the following decades and were widely interpreted as offering different theoretical and political interpretations of the consequences of the migration to, and settlement in, Britain by British subjects and citizens from the Caribbean and the Indian subcontinent. And indeed they did offer very different analyses. Notably, Rex sought to reinterpret the concept of racism to ensure that it could encompass the then contemporary political discourse about immigration that avoided any direct references to an alleged hierarchy of "races" while at the same time referring to or implying the existence of different "races." Initially, Banton (1987) interpreted this shift in discourse as evidence of a decline in racism. This conclusion was to lead him to eventually reject the concept of racism entirely.

But, more remarkably, despite their very different philosophical and theoretical backgrounds and conclusions, they had something in common. Both Banton and Rex mirrored the language of everyday life, incorporated it into academic discourse, and thereby legitimated it. They agreed that Britain (which they both analyzed comparatively with reference to the United States and South Africa) had a "race relations" problem. Rex, in particular, wished to conceptualize this problem theoretically in the discipline of sociology. In so doing, both premised their arguments on the understanding that scientific knowledge proves that "races" do not exist in the sense widely understood in everyday commonsense discourse: if "race" was a problem, it was a social and not a biological problem, one rooted in part at least in the continued popular belief in the existence of "races." Indeed, John Rex had been on the team of experts recruited by UNESCO to officially discredit the continuing exploitation of nineteenth-century scientific knowledge about "race" by certain political groups and to educate public opinion by making widely known the more recent conclusions of biological and genetic scientists (Montagu 1972).

The concept of "race relations" seemed to have impeccable credentials, unlike the language of "dark strangers," for example. This is in part because the notion was borrowed from the early sociology of the

"Chicago School" in the United States, which, among other things, was interested in the consequences of the early-twentieth-century migration from the southern to the northern states of "Negroes" fleeing poverty (and much else) in search of wage labor alongside the continuing large-scale migration from Europe to the United States. As a result of the former migration, "Negro" and "white races" entered, so sociologists conceptualized, into conflicting social relations in the burgeoning industrial urban areas of the northern states. Thus was born a new field of study in sociology. Colored migration to British cities after 1945 provided an opportunity for sociologists to import this field of study into Britain. Britain, too, now had a "race relations" problem.

Moreover, for Rex at least, "race relations situations" were by definition characterized by the presence of a racist ideology. Hence, the struggle against colonialism could now be pursued within the Mother Country "herself." By intervening in the new, domestic "race relations" problem on the side of the colonized victims, one could position oneself against the British state by opposing the introduction of immigration controls intended specifically to prevent "colored" British subjects from entering Britain. Such was the rush to be on the side of "the angels" that few, if any, wondered what they looked like or even whether there was any validity in the very concept of "angel."

There was a further import from the United States that had a substantial impact on the everyday and academic discourses of "race relations" in the late 1960s and early 1970s in Britain. The struggle for civil rights and against racism on the part of "the blacks" in the United States (the notion of "Negro" was now past its shelf life and, like "colored" before it, had been consigned to the waste-basket of politically unacceptable language) had the effect of mobilizing not only many "blacks" in Britain but also many "whites" politically inclined toward one of several competing versions of socialist transformation. And, if radical "blacks" were busy seizing the moment in the name of antiracism and "black autonomy," there was little political or academic space within which radically inclined "white" social scientists could wonder about the legitimacy and the consequences of seizing the language of "race" to do battle against racism. For it was specifically in the name of "race" that "black" people were resisting their long history of colonial oppression. Indeed, in some versions of this vision of liberation, contemporary "blacks" were the direct descendants and inheritors of the African "race" which had been deceived and disinherited by the "white devils" many centuries ago. In this "race war," the "white race" was soon to face the Day of Judgment.

Possession of a common language and associated historical traditions can blind as well as illuminate. It is especially significant that both the Left and the Right in Britain looked across the Atlantic when seeking to analyze and to offer forecasts about the outcome of the "race relations" problem that both agreed existed in Britain. The infamous speeches on immigration made by Member of Parliament Enoch Powell in the late 1960s and 1970s contained vivid images refracting then-contemporary events in cities in the United States and framing them as prophecies of what would inevitably happen in English cities if the "alien wedge" was not quickly "repatriated." At the same time the Left drew political inspiration from the "black" struggle against racism and sought to incorporate aspects of its rhetoric, style, and politics. Hence, while there was disagreement about the identity of the heroes and villains of "race relations" in the United States, there was fundamental agreement that "race relations" in the United States provided a framework within which to assess the course of "race relations" in Britain. Even legislation intended to regulate "race relations" and to make racialized discrimination illegal refracted the "American experience."

As a result, the academic and political responses to the "race relations" problem in Britain were largely isolated from the situation elsewhere in Europe, particularly in northwest Europe which was experiencing a quantitatively more substantial migration than that taking place in Britain. Two features are pertinent to the argument here. First, the nation-states of northwest Europe had recently experienced either fascist rule or fascist occupation and therefore the direct consequences of the so-called "final solution to the Jewish question" which sought to eliminate the "Jewish race." Hence, the collective historical memory of most of the major cities of northwest Europe was shaped by the genocide effected against the Jews and legitimated in the name of "race," even if that historical memory was now the focus of denial or repression. Second, this experience left the collective memory especially susceptible to the activities of UNESCO and others seeking to discredit the idea of "race" as a valid and meaningful descriptor. Hence, the temporal and spatial proximity of the Holocaust rendered its legitimating racism (a racism in which the idea of "race" was explicit and central) an immediate reality. In this context, few people were willing to make themselves vulnerable to the charge of racism. Suppressing the idea of "race," at least in the official and formal arenas of public life, became a political imperative.

The political and academic culture of mainland northwest Europe has, therefore, been open to two developments which distinguish it from that existing in the islands that lie to the north of the coast of France. First, in any debate about the scope and validity of the concept of racism, the Jewish experience of racism is much more likely to be discussed and even to be prioritized over any other. Second, the idea of "race" itself became highly sensitive politically. Its very use as a descriptor is more likely to be interpreted as evidence of racist beliefs. As a result, the idea is rarely employed in everyday political and academic discussion, at least not in connection with domestic social relations. However, in Britain, given the combination of the colonial migration and the multiple ideological exchanges with the United States, there were far fewer constraints on the everyday use of the idea of "race" and on a redefinition of the concept of racism. The latter came to refer exclusively to an ideology held by "white" people about "black" people, rooted in capitalist expansion beyond Europe and colonial exploitation.

Having recognized the relative distinctiveness of the political and academic space in northwest Europe and then having occupied that space, one can view those social relations defined in Britain and the United States as "race relations" from another point of view, for there is no public or academic reference to the existence of "race relations" in contemporary France or Germany. It then becomes possible to pose questions that seem not to be posed from within these intimately interlinked social and historical contexts. What kinds of social relations are signified as "race relations"? Why is the idea of "race" employed in everyday life to refer only to certain groups of people and only to certain social situations? And why do social scientists unquestioningly import everyday meanings into their reasoning and theoretical frameworks in defining "race" and "race relations" as a particular field of study? What does it mean for an academic to claim, for example, that "race" is a factor in determining the structure of social inequality, or that "race" and gender are interlinked forms of oppression? What is intended and what might be the consequences of asserting as an academic that "race matters"?

These are the kinds of questions that Miles has been posing since the 1980s (e.g., Miles 1982, 1984, 1989), influenced in part by the French theorist Guillaumin (1972, 1995). The answers to these questions lead to the conclusion that one should follow the example of biological and genetic scientists and refuse to attribute analytical status to the *idea* of "race" within the social sciences and thereby refuse to use it as a descriptive and explanatory *concept*. The reasoning can be summarized as follows (cf. Miles 1982, 22–43; 1993, 47–49).

First, the idea of "race" is used to effect reification within sociological analysis insofar as the outcome of an often complex social process is explained as the consequence of something named "race" rather than of the social process itself. Consider the publication of *The Bell Curve* by Richard J. Herrnstein and Charles Murray (1994) and the authors' common assertion that "race" determines academic performance and life chances. The assertion can be supported with statistical evidence that demonstrates that, in comparison with "black people," "white people" are more likely to achieve top grades in school and to enter leading universities in the United States. The determining processes are extremely complex, including among other things parental class position and active and passive racialized stereotyping and exclusion in the classroom and beyond. The effects of these processes are all mediated via a prior racialized categorization into a "black-white" dichotomy that is employed in everyday social relations. Hence, it is not "race" that determines academic performance: rather, academic performance is determined by the interplay of social processes, one of which is premised on the articulation of racism to effect and legitimate exclusion. Indeed, given the nineteenth-century meanings of "race," this form of reification invites the possibility of explaining academic performance as the outcome of some quality within the body of those racialized as "black."

Second, when academics who choose to write about "race relations" seek to speak to a wider audience (an activity which we believe to be fully justified) or when their writings are utilized by nonacademics, their use unwittingly legitimates and reinforces everyday beliefs that the human species is constituted by a number of different "races," each of which is characterized by a particular combination of real or imagined physical features or marks and cultural practices. When West seeks to persuade the "American public" that "Race Matters," there is no doubt that he himself does not believe in the existence of biologically defined "races." But he cannot control the meanings attributed to his claim on the part of those who identify differences in skin color, for example, as marks designating the existence of "blacks" and "whites" as discrete "races." Unintentionally, his writing may thus come to serve as a legitimation not only of a belief in the existence of "race" as a biological phenomenon but also of racism itself. He could avoid this outcome by breaking with the "race relations" paradigm.

Third, as a result of reification and the interplay between academic and commonsense discourses, the use of "race" as an analytical concept can incorporate into the discourse of antiracism a notion that has been central to the evolution of racism. Antiracist activities promote the idea that "races" really exist as biological categories of people. Thus, while challenging the legitimation of unequal treatment and the stereotyping implicit and explicit in racism, the reproduction within antiracist campaigns of the idea that there are real biological differences creating groups of human beings sustains in the public consciousness the ideological precondition for stereotyping and unequal treatment. In other words, use of the idea of "race" provides one of the conditions for the reproduction of racism within the discourse and practice of antiracism.

For these reasons, the idea of "race" should not be employed as an analytical category within the social sciences. It follows that the object of study should not be described as "race relations." To reiterate, while we reject the "race relations" problematic for the analysis of racism, we do not reject the concept of racism. Rather, we critique the "race relations" problematic in order to recognize the existence of a plurality of historically specific racisms, not all of which explicitly employ the idea of "race." In contrast, the "race relations" paradigm refers exclusively to either "black-white" social relations or to social relations between "people of color" and "white people." This allows for only one racism, the racism of "whites," which has as its object and victim "people of color" (e.g., Essed 1991).

Moreover, as the academic literature of the 1990s recognizes, many recent and contemporary discourses which eschew use of the idea of "race" nevertheless advance notions that were previously a referent of the "idea" of "race." We can only comprehend contemporary discourses that dispense with the explicit use of the idea of "race" and those that naturalize and inferiorize "white" populations by rescuing the concept of racism from the simultaneous inflation and narrowing of its meaning by the intersection of the academic and political debate in Britain and the United States since the end of World War II.

Reflections on the Racialization of the United States by the American Academy

A number of observations may be made about the contemporary academic debate about racism in the U.S. analytical position and from Europe. First, when compared with the mid- and late 1960s, the debate about racism is now an extremely contested one, in which many voices are arguing different positions. On the one hand, writers such as David Wellman (1993) continue to assert that racism remains the primary determinant of social inequality in the United States. On the other hand, writers such as William Julius Wilson (1980, 1987, 1999) posit that the significance of class (or, more specifically, class differentiation) has increased and is now far more salient than "race" in determining the life chances of African Americans.[1] Between these two positions, one finds writers such as West who assert that the continuing impact of racism has to be assessed in terms of its relationship with the effects of class, sexism, and homophobia (e.g., 1994, 44). Moreover, the voices of "Afrocentrists" (e.g., Karenga 1993), "black feminists" (e.g., hooks 1990; Guy-Sheftall 1995), and "critical race theorists" (Delgado 1995; Wing 1997, 2003) have become extremely influential in this debate over the last decade. At the same time a "black" conservative intellectual tradition has emerged and is attracting increasing attention (e.g., Sowell 1994; Faryna, Stetson, and Conti 1997).

Second, the debate either takes for granted or explicitly argues that racism refers to an ideology and (in some cases) a set of practices, of which "black" people are the exclusive victims: racism refers to what "white" people think about and do to "black" people. While the concept of institutional racism goes further by eschewing any reference to human intentionality, it retains the "black-white" dichotomy in order to identify beneficiary and victim. Thus the scope of the concept of racism is very narrowly defined. The centrality of the "black-white" dichotomy denies the possibility by definition that any group other than "white" people can articulate, practice, or benefit from racism and suggests that only "black people" can be the object or victim of racism.

Some of West's writing illustrates this difficulty. He clearly distinguishes himself from those he describes as black nationalists when he argues that their obsession with white racism obstructs the development of the political alliances that are essential to effecting social changes that will alleviate the suffering of black people in the United States and that white racism alone cannot explain the socioeconomic position of the majority of black Americans (1994, 82, 98–99). Moreover, he argues that certain black nationalist accounts "simply mirror the white supremacist ideals we are opposing" (1994, 99). Yet, he seems reluctant to identify any form of racism other than white racism. In his carefully considered discussion of what he describes as "Black-Jewish relations," he distinguishes between black anti-Semitism and Jewish anti-black racism (1994, 104; see also Lerner and West 1995, 135–56), which suggests that these are qualitatively different phenomena: Jews can be racist while Afro-Americans can be anti-Semitic. This interpretation is reinforced by his assertion that black anti-Semitism is a form of "xenophobia from below" which has a different institutional power than "those racisms that afflict their victims from above" (1994, 109–10) even though both merit moral condemnation.

A similar distinction is implicit in the writing of Robert Blauner (1992) who, partly in response to the arguments posed by Miles, has revised his position significantly since the 1960s. Blauner returns to the common distinction between "race" and ethnicity, arguing that the "peculiarly modern division of the world into a discrete number of hierarchically ranked races is a historic product of Western colonialism" (Blauner 1992, 61). This, he argues, is a very different process from that associated with ethnicity. Hence Blauner refrains from analyzing the ideologies employed to justify the exclusion of Italians and Jews in the United States in the 1920s as racism: these populations were "white ethnics" who were "viewed racially" (64). Concerning the period of fascism in Germany, Blauner refers to genocide "where racial imagery was obviously intensified" (64), but presumably the imagery could never be intensified to the point of warranting description as racism because the Jews were not "black." Yet, as we shall see shortly when we examine West, Blauner comes very close to breaking with the "race relations" problematic when he argues, "Much of the popular discourse about race in America today goes awry because ethnic realities get lost under the racial umbrella. The positive meanings and potential of ethnicity are overlooked, even overrun, by the more inflammatory meanings of race" (61).

Third, the debate is firmly grounded in the specific realities of the history and contemporary social structure of the United States or, rather, a particular interpretation of those realities. It is perhaps not surprising, therefore, that scholars of racism in the United States have shown so little interest in undertaking comparative research. There are important exceptions. Some scholars have compared the United States with South

Africa (e.g., Van den Berghe 1978; Fredrickson 1981, 1995, 1997; for a recent study, see Marx 1998); and a comparison between the United States and England achieved some prominence in the 1970s (Katznelson 1976; for a recent analysis, see Small 1994). However, most U.S. scholars of racism focus on the United States itself. This may, perhaps, be explained as the outcome of a benign ethnocentrism; but it could also be a function of the limited scope of a theory of racism, which in turn is closely tied to the "race relations" paradigm by means of a racialized dualism that bifurcates the United States into "blacks" and "whites." The corollary is that racism is considered to be exclusively a condition or effect of a society structured by a racialized dualism. Such a theoretical position has limited its use to the analysis of social formations where there is no "black" presence.

Yet there is evidence of an increasingly conscious unease with this "race relations" paradigm and the "black-white" dichotomy. For example, as we have already noted, West argues "race matters." "Race is the most explosive issue in American life precisely because it forces us to confront the tragic facts of poverty and paranoia, despair and distrust" (1994, 155–56). But he also argues that it is necessary to formulate new frameworks and languages in order to comprehend the current crisis in the United States and to identify solutions to it (1994, 11). Indeed, he asserts that it is imperative to move beyond the narrow framework of "dominant liberal and conservative views of race in America," which have a "worn-out vocabulary" (1994, 4). West does not seem to accept the idea that "race" itself is an example of this exhausted language for he employs it throughout without hesitation, despite his belief that the manner in which "we set up the terms for discussing racial issues shapes our perception and response to these issues" (1994, 6). Later in the book he seems to be on the verge of following the logic of this argument through to its ultimate conclusion when he argues that the Clarence Thomas–Anita Hill hearings demonstrate that "the very framework of racial reasoning" needs to be called into question in order to reinterpret the black freedom struggle not as an issue of "skin pigmentation and racial phenotype" but as one of ethics and politics (1994, 38). And yet he does not follow through to the point of acknowledging that there cannot be a place for the use of the idea of "race" as an analytical concept in the social sciences.

But there is a transatlantic trade in theories of racism, which is now two-way. Some scholars in the United States have taken note of debates and arguments generated in Europe, including contributions that question some of the key assumptions that characterize the debate. Some of these writers have also acknowledged and responded to Miles's criticisms regarding the use of the idea of "race" as an analytical concept and the way in which the concept of racism has been inflated (Miles 1982, 1989, 1993). Recent contributions by Wellman (1993), Blauner (1992), Omi and Winant (1993, 1994), Winant (1994), and Goldberg (1993) all refer to and comment on these arguments, with varying degrees of enthusiasm. Interestingly, they all seem to ignore the writing of Lieberman and his associates (e.g., Lieberman 1968; Reynolds 1992) in the United States who argue for a position which overlaps in important respects with that outlined here.

Goldberg offers perhaps the most complex and thoughtful response in the course of a wide-ranging and philosophically inspired analysis and conceptual language required to analyze contemporary racism.[2] His use of racialized discourse as a theoretical framework for understanding and explaining racism across different historical contexts is both useful and original.[3] However, we will focus here on the work of Omi and Winant, in part because their writing has already had considerable influence in both the United States and Britain, and in part because some of their key concepts have parallels in the equally influential work of Gilroy (1987).[4] Omi and Winant's influence is well deserved, for there is much to learn from their theoretical and conceptual innovations.

Although we prefer to employ a concept of racialized (rather than racial) formation, we agree that racialized categories are socially created, transformed, and destroyed through historical time (Omi and Winant 1994, 55). We, too, recognize that it is essential to distinguish between "race" (although we do not use "race" as a *concept* but, rather, we capture its use in everyday life by referring to the *idea* of "race") and the concept of racism, a distinction that allows us to further distinguish between racialization and racism.[5] We also agree that it is essential to retain the concept of racism (Wellman is simply mistaken when he claims that Miles argues that racism is not a useful concept: 1993, 3) to identify a multiplicity of historically specific racisms, with the consequence that there is "nothing inherently white about racism" (Omi and Winant 1994, 72).[6]

It is important to highlight these areas of agreement prior to considering Omi and Winant's defense of the use of the idea of "race" as an analytical concept in the social sciences. Although they have stimulated in-novations within the discussion about racism in the United States, we maintain that they have failed to pursue the logic of these innovations to their ultimate conclusion. Their emphasis upon the way in which the idea of "race" has been socially constructed and reconstructed has stimulated debate in the United States about the theoretical and analytical status of the idea of "race."

Other scholars in the United States have made important contributions to the development of this debate, notably Lieberman (1968, 2003), Fields (1990, 2001), Roediger (1994, 1998), and most recently Appiah (1996). As stated in the introduction to this volume, Fields's work is es-pecially relevant in this context because she reaches a conclusion that ac-cords closely with that articulated by Miles (see Miles 1982; 1993, 27–52). Omi and Winant have criticized Fields's conclusions in the course of defending their continued use of "race" as an analytical concept, and it is therefore appropriate to reflect upon the arguments and evidence that they have employed. Omi and Winant offer two criticisms of the position that the idea of "race" should be analyzed exclusively as a social or ide-ological construct (1993, 5). First, they suggest that such an understand-ing fails to recognize the social consequences of the longevity of the con-cept of "race." Second, they claim that, as a result of this longevity, "race is an almost indissoluble part of our identities," a fact that is not recog-nized by those who argue that "race" is an ideological construct.

We contend that they are mistaken on both counts. Miles (1982, 1993) highlights the historical evolution of the meanings attributed to the idea of "race" and, for example in his discussions of colonialism and of the ar-ticulation between racism and nationalism, demonstrates the centrality of the idea of belonging to the "white race" to the construction of the iden-tity of the British bourgeoisie and working class. Indeed, these claims can be refuted simply by citing a quotation from Fields that Omi and Winant themselves reproduce (1993, 5). Fields (1990) writes,

> Nothing handed down from the past could keep race alive if we did not constantly reinvent and re-ritualize it to fit our own terrain. If race lives on today, it can do so only because we continue to create and re-create it in our social life, continue to verify it, and thus continue to need a social vocabulary that will allow us to make sense, not of what our ancestors did then, but of what we choose to do now. (118)

Fields certainly does not deny that, in the contemporary world, people use the idea of "race" to classify themselves and others into social collectivities and act in ways consistent with such a belief to collectively produce structured exclusion. Hence, Omi and Winant's critique is shown to be vacuous. Fields's key objective is to critique the way in which historians invoke the idea of "race" to construct explanations for events and processes in the past, and her critique applies equally to the work of sociologists such as Omi and Winant who have reinvented and reritualized the idea of "race" to fit their own terrain within the academy (which is, after all, only one more arena of social life).

Let us examine how Omi and Winant reinvent and thereby reify the idea of "race" in the course of their sociological analysis. Consider the following claim: "One of the first things we notice about people when we meet them (along with their sex) is their race" (1994, 59). Elsewhere, they argue, "To be raceless is akin to being genderless. Indeed, when one cannot identify another's race, a microsociological 'crisis of interpretation' results" (1993, 5). How are we to interpret this assertion? While they also claim that "race is . . . a socially constructed way of differentiating human beings" (1994, 65), the former assertion is at the very least open to interpretation as suggesting that "race" is an objective quality inherent in a person's being, that every human being is a member of a "race," and that such membership is inscribed in a person's visible appearance. It is in the interstices of such ambiguity that the idea of "race" as a biological fact does not just "live on" but is actively re-created by social scientists in the course of their academic practice.

This argument sometimes stimulates incomprehension on the part of U.S. scholars who echo arguments employed in some critiques of this position in Britain. It is often said, "How can you deny analytical status to the idea of race and ultimately the existence of race when blacks and whites are so obviously different and when all the evidence demonstrates that their life chances differ too?" In responding to this question, it is necessary first to problematize what it takes for granted, specifically that the "black-white" division is *obvious*. The quality of *obviousness* is not inherent in a phenomenon but is the outcome of a social process in the course of which meaning is attributed to the phenomenon in a particular historical and social context. Those who are its subject and object learn the meaning. They therefore learn to habitually recognize it and perhaps to pass on this signification and knowledge to others, with the result that the quality of obviousness attributed to the phenomenon is reproduced through historical time and social space.

Skin color is one such phenomenon. Its visibility is not inherent in its existence but is a product of signification: human beings identify skin color to *mark* or symbolize other phenomena in a historical context in which other significations occur. When human practices include and exclude people in the light of the signification of skin color, collective identities are produced and social inequalities are structured. It is for this reason that historical studies of the meanings attributed to skin color in different historical contexts and through time are of considerable importance. And it is in relation to such studies that one can inquire into the continuities and discontinuities with contemporary processes of signification that sustain the obviousness of skin color as a social *mark*. Historically and contemporarily, differences in skin color have been and are signified as a mark that suggests the existence of different "races." But people do not see "race"; rather, they observe certain combinations of real and sometimes imagined somatic and cultural characteristics, to which they attribute meaning with the idea of "race." Furthermore, a difference of skin color is not essential to the process of marking; other somatic features can be and are signified in order to racialize. Indeed, in some historical circumstances, the absence of somatic difference has been central to the powerful impact of racism: the racialized "enemy within" may be identified as an even more threatening presence if the group is not "obviously different" because "they" can then be imagined to be everywhere.

Omi and Winant reify this social process and reach the conclusion that all human beings belong to a "race" because they seek to construct their analytical *concepts* to reproduce directly the commonsense ideologies of the everyday world. Because the idea of "race" continues to be widely used in everyday life in the United States (and Britain) to classify human beings and to interpret their behavior, Omi and Winant believe that social scientists should employ a *concept* of race. This assumption is the source of our disagreement with them. We believe that one of the contemporary challenges in the analysis of racisms is to develop a conceptual vocabulary that explicitly acknowledges that people use the *idea* of "race" in the everyday world while resisting the use of the idea of "race" as an analytical *concept* when social scientists analyze the discourses and practices of the everyday world. It is not the *concept* of "race" that "continues to play a fundamental role in structuring and representing the social world" (Omi and Winant 1994, 55) but the *idea* of "race." The task of social scientists is to develop a theoretical framework for the analysis of this process of structuring and representing "race" which breaks completely with the reified language of biological essentialism. Hence, we object to Omi and Winant's project of developing a critical theory of the *concept* of "race" because we also recognize the importance of historical context and contingency in the framing of racialized categories and the social construction of racialized experiences (Omi and Winant 1993). We believe that historical context requires us to criticize all concepts of "race," and that this can be done by means of a concept of racialization (Miles 1989, 73–77). Omi and Winant's defense of the concept of "race" is a classic example of the way in which the academy in the United States continues to racialize the world.

Furthermore, the concept of racialization employed by Omi and Winant is not fully developed and is not used in a sustained analytical manner. This is because it is grounded in "race relations" sociology, a sociology that reifies the notion of "race" and thereby implies the existence of "racial groups" as biological categories. Additionally, they fail to take into account the interplay between the social relations of production and the racialization process. We argue that the process of racialization takes place and has its effects in the context of class and production relations and that the idea of "race" may indeed not even be explicitly articulated in this process (Miles 1989, 1993).

Bringing Class Back In

The collapse of the communist project in central and eastern Europe, in conjunction with the fashionable predominance of postmodern theory, resulted in a "retreat from class" in sociological analysis during the 1990s (Wood 1996). To reassert the importance of class and production relations in relation to the process of racialization may, therefore, be viewed as an attempt to return to an outdated theoretical paradigm. But Marxist theory has always been a site of conflicting and competing readings of Marx. The Stalinist project certainly died with the collapse of communism, but other readings of Marx, other traditions of Marxist theory, can offer an explanation for what happened in central and eastern Europe in the late 1980s and the early 1990s. Moreover, much of the language and subject matter of postmodern theory presumes an explanation for the increasing importance of contingency, ambiguous and plural identities, the dissolution of the nation-state, and that complex of social transformations summarized in the concept of globalization. We do not intend to be simply mischievous by suggesting that there are several useful insights into these very processes in that classic rallying cry to class struggle, *The Communist Manifesto*. More detailed investigations by contemporary analysts working within the tradition of political economy testify to the continuing vigor and power of this tradition of analysis (e.g., Balibar and Wallerstein 1991).

The necessary reevaluation of the nature of class analysis in the light of, for example, feminist theory, among other critical interventions, are not the substance of this book. But it is important to continue to draw attention to the importance of class in an analysis of the racialization process. The gendered subjects and objects of the racialization process continue to be differentially located in the structures of capitalist relations of production.

A Racism of Another Color?

West begins his first essay in *Race Matters* with a reference to the Los Angeles riots of April 1992. He denies that they were either a "race riot or a class rebellion." Rather,

> this monumental upheaval was a multi-racial, trans-class, and largely male display of social rage. Of those arrested, only 36 percent were black, more than a third had full-time jobs, and most claimed to shun political affiliation. What we witnessed in Los Angeles was the consequence of a lethal linkage of economic decline, cultural decay, and political lethargy in American life. Race was the visible catalyst, not the underlying cause. (1994, 3–4)

He concludes by claiming that the meaning of the riots is obscured because we are trapped by the narrow framework imposed by the dominant views of "race" in the United States.

The *Los Angeles Times* Opinion Editor rendered a different version of the narrow framework of the "black-white" dichotomy. In an essay in the October 1992 issue of the *Atlantic Monthly* entitled "Blacks vs. Browns,"

Jack Miles suggested that Latinos were taking jobs that the nation, by dint of the historic crimes committed against them, owed to African Americans. He blamed Latinos for the poverty in African American communities—a gross misattribution of responsibility—while reinforcing "race" as a relevant analytical and social category. His confusion was revealing; the "two societies, one black, one white—separate and unequal" dichotomy articulated by de Tocqueville and made famous by the 1968 report of the National Advisory Commission on Civil Disorders cannot provide an analytical framework to deconstruct the post-Fordist[7] racialized social relations of the 1990s. The meaning of West's argument is constructed as much by what is not said as by what is. He is silent about the definition of "race riot" and what specific events would be classified as a matter of "race." Presumably, the events of April 1992 would have been a "race riot" if the principal actors had been "blacks" and "whites." Hence, West refers to "race" only as the visible catalyst. Rodney King was "obviously black" and the police officers that arrested him were "obviously white." But the riots themselves did not fit the "race relations" paradigm because the rioters and those who became the victims of the riot were not exclusively "blacks" and "whites."

Indeed, as the media were framing the events of April 1992 in "black-white" terms in the great melodrama of "race relations," the first image across the airwaves was that of men atop a car waving the Mexican flag. Thus, "Hispanic" may signify as presumptively "white" in the social dynamics that rest on a system of neat, racialized categories, but this has little to do with the popular understanding and experience of Latinos. We believe the analytical task is, therefore, to explain the complex nature of the structural changes associated with the emergence of the "post-Fordist" socioeconomic landscape and the reconfigured racialized social relations in Los Angeles specifically and in the United States and beyond more generally (see Valle and Torres 1998).

As a simple measure of these reconfigured social relations, consider the following. Perhaps half the businesses looted or burned during the Los Angeles riots were owned by Korean Americans and another third or so were owned by Mexican Americans or Latinos and Cuban Americans. Those engaged in looting and burning certainly included Afro-Americans; but poor, recent, and often undocumented immigrants and refugees from Mexico and Central America were equally prominent. Of those arrested, 51 percent were Latinos and 36 percent were African Americans. And of those who died in the civil unrest, about half were

African Americans and about a third were Latinos. All this is surprising only if one begins with the assumption that the events were or could have been "race riots" in the sense that became hegemonic in the 1960s.

Such an assumption is problematic for two reasons. First, academics, media reporters, and politicians "conspired" to use the vocabulary of "race" to make sense of the Los Angeles riots because "race" is a central component of everyday commonsense discourse in the United States. When it became overwhelmingly apparent that it was not a "black-white" riot, the language of "race" was, nevertheless, unthinkingly retained by switching to the notion of "multiracial" in order to encompass the diverse historical and cultural origins of the participants and victims. Thus, while the "race relations" paradigm was dealt a serious blow by the reality of the unrest, the vocabulary of "race" was retained. But this is where we find the source of West's unease, for the idea of "race" is so firmly embedded in common sense that it cannot easily encompass a reference to "Koreans" or "Hispanics" or "Latinos," for these groups are neither "black" nor "white." It is thus not surprising then that pundits and scholars stumble over "racial" ambiguity. The clash of racialized language with a changing political economy clearly presents challenges for scholars and activists alike.

Second, if one had begun with an analysis grounded simultaneously in history and political economy rather than with the supremely ideological notion of "race relations," one would have quickly concluded that the actors in any riot in central Los Angeles would probably be *ethnically* diverse. Large-scale inward migration from Mexico and Central America and from Southeast Asia into California has coincided with a restructuring of the California economy, the loss of major manufacturing jobs, and large-scale internal migration within the urban sprawl of "greater" Los Angeles. Consequently, the spatial, ethnic, and class structures that underlay the Watts riots of 1965 have been transformed into a much more complex set of relationships. The most general conditions were structural in nature, and thus the decline and shift in the manufacturing base in Los Angeles was not unique but represented a shift in the mode of capital accumulation worldwide. As Valle and Torres (2000) suggest, the "uprising" of 1992 not only represented a material and discursive turn in "race relations" but the end of traditional African American politics in Los Angeles, along with the promise of a class-based coalition politics in the Latino metropolis.

In order to analyze these new racialized relations, we do not need to employ a concept of "race." Indeed, its retention is a significant hindrance. But we do need to draw upon the insights consequent upon the creation of the concept of *racisms*. The complex relationships of exploitation and resistance, grounded in differences of class, gender, and ethnicity, give rise to a multiplicity of ideological constructions of the racialized "Other." For, while the idea of "race" does not matter outside the process of racialization to which academics are active contributors, the racisms articulated in Los Angeles and elsewhere in order to naturalize, inferiorize, exclude, and sustain privilege and growing class inequality, certainly do matter.

2

Racialized Metropolis

Theorizing Asian American and Latino Identities and Ethnicities in Southern California

with ChorSwang Ngin

When you say "America" you refer to the territory stretching between the icecaps of the two poles. So to hell with your barriers and frontier guards! (Diego Rivera, cited in Davis 2001)

Young Suk Lee is a Korean fashion retailer in the garment district in Los Angeles. Like other retailers in Los Angeles, she hires local Latinas as sales clerks and serves a largely English and Spanish-speaking clientele.[1] According to the U.S. Census Bureau, she is classified under the Asian Pacific "race" category. Americans in general perceive her as another immigrant ethnic-entrepreneur success story. However, to her these labels are irrelevant. Her biggest concern is her inability to speak English, having grown up speaking Spanish in Peru. In 1990, she left her Latin American homeland to work in a relative's fashion business in Los Angeles. Now she is considering whether to remain in the United States to invest in an accessory store in the new development along 11th and Maple or whether to join a relative in another business venture located in the fashionable business district near the Lotte Hotel in Seoul, Korea.

Although "race" and "ethnicity" have long been key concepts in sociological discourse and public debate, they remain problematic. Policy pundits, journalists, and conservative and liberal academics alike work within categories of "race" and "ethnicity" in a theoretical framework of unanimity in relation to their analytical value. Racialized group conflicts are framed and advanced as a "race relations" problem and are presented to the public mostly in black and white terms.[2]

In 2002, the Latino population of Los Angeles County was 4.3 million, or 44 percent. A significant portion of the Latino population were immigrants from Central America and Mexico during the 1980s. In 2002, the total of the various Asian subgroup populations in Los Angeles County was 1.3 million, or 12 percent of the county. However, not all groups have experienced growth. The county's African American population has remained less steady at about 930,000, just under 10 percent. By 2005, the African American population is expected to decline slightly to 8 percent of the county total. Thirty-six percent of the residents of L.A. County are foreign born, and the largest group of immigrants is from Latin America at 62 percent, followed by 30 percent from Asian countries.

The ethnic transformation of Los Angeles is occurring during a period of massive cuts in aid to housing, schools, and social services. The passage of Proposition 187 and the California "Civil Rights" Initiative represent the politics of resentment in a period of growing inequality in both individual earnings and family income (Allen and Turner 1997). The rich are getting richer, the middle class is besieged by the threat of unemployment and rising debt levels, and the racialized poor, particularly young African American and Latino men, are either in state or federal prison or being killed.

A report released in 1998 by the California Assembly Select Committee on the California Middle Class, chaired by Assemblyman Wally Knox, indicated that income inequality in Los Angeles has increased significantly. The study on which the report was based found that as of 1996, 41 percent of the residents of Los Angeles County lived in households with annual incomes below $20,000, and fully two-thirds lived in households with annual incomes below $40,000. Only 26 percent were in middle-income households making between $40,000 and $100,000, with 8 percent in households making more than $100,000.[3]

California's recovery from the recession of the early 1990s has not mitigated this trend but rather has magnified the effect of structural inequalities in the economy of Los Angeles. According to an analysis undertaken by the *Los Angeles Times* in 1999, nearly all the job growth in Los Angeles County, since the low point of the recession in the winter of 1993, has been in low-income jobs. Although the number of new jobs created is impressive, almost 300,000 since 1993, very few of these jobs fall in the middle-class income range of $40,000 to $60,000. The economic recovery of Los Angeles has produced far more parking lot attendants, waiters, and video store clerks than highly paid workers in information technology, entertainment, or international trade. The majority of new jobs pay less than $25,000 per year, and barely one new job in ten averages $60,000 per year.

The impact of these low salary figures is even more dramatic in light of the high cost of living in Los Angeles County. The high cost of real estate in Los Angeles makes it difficult for low-income workers to buy homes even if several wage earners share the same household. Whereas neighboring Orange County has seen a 10 percent increase in its home ownership rate in the 1990s, the rate for Los Angeles County has scarcely moved in the same period. Many of these new jobs also lack long-term security or health care benefits. According to Mark Drays, Research Director of the nonprofit Economic Roundtable, the net effect is that the population is "becoming more polarized."

The current socioeconomic condition of Latinos and Asian Americans in metropolitan Los Angeles can be traced to the emergence of the global economy. Such consequences highlight the need for scholars to link the condition of U.S. Latinos and Asian Americans in cities to the globalization of the economy. Few scholars have contributed more to our understanding of globalization and economic restructuring than Saskia Sassen (1996, 1998), who posits, "Trends in major cities cannot be understood in isolation of fundamental changes in the broader organization of advanced economies. The combination of economic, political, and technical forces that has contributed to the decline of mass production as the central element in the economy brought about a decline in a wider institutional framework that shaped the employment relations" (Sassen 1996, 590). In light of this view, theorizing about Asian American and Latino identities and ethnicities can be best understood in the context of the changing U.S. political economy and the new international division of labor.

The intent here is to problematize the notion of "race" and the related concept of "race relations" in terms of contemporary discourses on racialized identities and ethnicities in Southern California. As mentioned earlier, the ideas of "race" and "race relations" have been questioned analytically since the 1980s in British academic discourse (Miles 1982, 1989, 1993), and it is only recently that some U.S. scholars have also begun to consider the rationale and implications of that critique

(Goldberg 1990, 1995; Hune 1995; Miles and Torres 1999; Omi 1993; Small 1999; Torres and Ngin 1995).[4]

In our analysis of the Latino and Asian American populations in California, we advocate expanding the contemporary American debate by arguing for a complete rejection of the terms "race" and "race relations" in academic and public discourses. By introducing an alternative model that applies the concept of racialization to the California Asian and Latino populations and by recognizing racialization as the underlying factor in social relations, we can better understand the process of signification of one group by another and racialized struggles and tensions. This reexamination, stripped of "race" language, reveals the role of ethnicity and ethnic politics in shaping the discourse of "race." It further unveils a social relationship structured by deindustrialization, globalization, economic restructuring, and other considerations that determine social relations. Finally, this emphasis on the constant process of racialization attempts to conceptualize an ongoing social project attributing meaning to the use of "race" as a category of exclusion as well as resistance. By rejecting the notion of "race," this mode of analysis allows us to rescue racism from a focus on "race relations" issues. Our theorizing is situated in the spaces outside the dominant debate on "black and white" as well as outside the established disciplines of Asian American studies and Latino/Chicano studies. It is by thus critically questioning mainstream assumptions that we wish to theorize about Asian American and Latino ethnicity and identity and racialized relations in a changing megalopolis.

Revisioning the Paradigm

Numerous writers of American history have noted the centrality of a "black-white" paradigm in the American psyche. Yet, despite a substantial increase in the Latino and Asian populations, major debates on social policy continue to be grounded in black and white terms, albeit with glib references to "disenfranchised" Asian and Latino groups. A few examples include discussions on the American Dream (Carnoy 1994; Hochchild 1995), on the question of justice and "multicultural" democracy (hooks 1995; Marable 1995), and on the question of social policy (Steinberg 1995). With rare exceptions, the dialogue remains focused on black-white relations with occasional discussions of Asian Americans and

Latinos. Similarly, scholars whose opinions are sought after are either black or white. Intellectuals such as Cornel West, bell hooks, Manning Marable, and Henry Louis Gates, for example, tell us "what they think should be rather than what is or is likely to be" (Fredrickson 1996, 18), thereby providing authoritative voices representing the African American community. On the other hand, few Asian Americans and Latinos have become well known in the public sphere because they are rarely granted access to popular media.[5]

The black-and-white idea of "race" has a tenacious hold on the American ethos. Black is black, and white is white. It is all very clear. The question pertaining to Asian Americans and Latinos within the black-white framework is: Are they black or white? Inasmuch as these two groups are located outside the dominant "race-relations" paradigm, the crucial question in theorizing Asian Americans and Latinos has been: Is "race" important?

In a published conversation between two intellectuals on the changing nature of the U.S. debate on "race" and identity, both Cornel West, author of *Race Matters,* and J. Jorge Klor de Alva, an anthropologist, objected "to the essentialized conception of race, [and] to the idea that differences are innate and outside history" (Klor de Alva, Shorris, and West 1996, 56). While recognizing that African Americans are "biological and cultural hybrids," West continues to identify himself as "black." Klor de Alva objects to this reductionism that "transformed everyone with one drop of African blood into black" (58). He reasons that this reductionism is a "powerful mechanism for causing diversity to disappear" and "has the capacity to blur the differences between cultural groups, [and] to construct them in such a way that they became insignificant and to fuse them into a new group . . . which didn't exist before. . . . [It is a phenomenon that] is not seen any place in the world" (58).

Klor de Alva's observation regarding the categorization of heterogeneous groups into single entities applies to all racialized groups in the United States. People of different European religious and cultural origins and descent who arrive in this country are collapsed into a "white" group (Kazal 1995). The diversity of Asian Americans and Latinos is similarly collapsed into "Asian Pacific" and "Hispanic" categories. The single "Asian Pacific" category includes such diverse groups as Chinese, Filipino, Japanese, Asian Indian, Korean, Vietnamese, Laotian, Thai, Cambodian, Hmong, Pakistani, Indonesian, Hawaiian, and people from the Pacific Islands of Micronesia and Polynesia (Lott 1993). The single

"Hispanic" category representing the Latino population includes Mexican Americans of the Southwest, the colonized subjects from Puerto Rico, refugees from Cuba, and recent immigrants and refugees from Mexico and Central and South America. Each of these subgroups is further divided along linguistic, religious, regional, and especially class lines. While some Asian Americans within a subethnic group are professionals, entrepreneurs, or managerial workers (Ong and Blumenberg 1997), others are refugees dependent on the state for welfare (Leadership Education for Asian Pacifics 1993).

The question of class and class structure is even more problematic among the Latino populations. The existence of a Chicano class structure predates the Mexican-American War of 1846–48 (Barrera 1979). Today's population includes the Chicano/Latino working class, petty bourgeoisie, recent immigrants from Mexico and Latin America, and the Chicano professional managerial class (Barrera 1984; Rodriguez 1996). However, few studies delineate this gradation of class divisions within Latino communities. Some Asian and Latino "immigrants" are direct descendants dating back several generations, while others are recent arrivals. Some segments of the population are concentrated in ethnic enclaves,[6] while others are dispersed in the suburbs. Yet in government definitions and public discourse, these groups are collapsed into single categories. Conflicts between groups and individuals across these categories, often having to do with competition for scarce resources in an urban setting, are framed as "race relations" problems.

Despite these varied and complex characteristics among both Asian Americans and Latinos, a distinction can be made between recent immigrants and the earlier groups. That is, the recent groups have not been subjected to the same harsh, legal, exclusionary practices and therefore do not share the lived historical memory of virulent racism. It is important to recognize this difference between the two groups' experiences with racism, because it determines how others perceive ethnicity and how the ethnic groups involved filter it internally. All immigrants, however, are also connected to their native countries by transnational economic, social, and cultural processes. The material forces that determine their migration, their present production relations, and their class positions are similarly determined by the larger social structure and the global economy. As noted by Valle and Torres (1994, 2000), much needs to be learned about the nature and meaning of Latino class relations in a "postindustrial" society and the way these divisions manifest themselves in the changing organization of work, urban politics, and relations with the state. The class diversity and different historical experiences of the immigrant population make representing them as single groups highly problematic if not untenable.[7]

The Racialization Model

The mistaken assumption about the language of the "race" and "race relations" paradigm has led many scholars to propose innovative ways of understanding social relations without reifying the notion of "race." Thus, a number of writers have carefully placed the term "race" in quotation marks to distinguish it from the word's biological connotation (Miles 1982; Small 1994; Smith 1989; Williams 1994). Miles's (1982, 1989) notion of racialization—the representation and definition of "Others" based on the signification of human biological characteristics—is particularly useful in understanding early U.S. discourse of non-European immigrants and natives. Until recently, discourse on Native Americans, African Americans, Latinos, and Asian Americans depended largely on a phenotypical representation and evaluation. Both color and physical appearance were given social significance. By reason of their color and physical features, these populations were perceived as bearers of disease and as endangering "American" morals and "racial" purity. This "race"-based discourse provided the ideological context, in part, for the enactment of past restrictive immigration laws and discriminatory policies. Examples of exclusionary public policies based on ideas of "race," color, or blood included the 1790 Act prohibiting "nonwhites" from becoming citizens, the 1854 *People v. Hall* case denying "Chinese and other people not white" from testifying against whites, the 1882 Chinese Exclusion Act, the 1922 *Ozawa* case denying a fully assimilated Japanese from becoming a citizen, and the 1923 *Thind* decision denying Asian Indians from becoming naturalized citizens (Chan 1991; Takaki 1989).

In elaborating Miles's original use of racialization[8] as it applies to a specific African American population, Stephen Small (1999) clarified that it is

a set of assumptions and key concepts which explore the multiple factors that shape what has previously been called "race relations." Some of these factors entail explicit reference to "race" [but] other factors—such as competition for economic and political resources . . . may seem to have no "racial" reference. The racialization problematic enables us to redefine the relationship between these seemingly unrelated variables and, importantly, begin to assess the significance of each. In sum, analysts working within the racialization problematic are able to ask the question: "If 'race relations' are not the relationship between biologically different 'races,' then what are they?" (49)

In recent years, Ngin (1995) has also diligently avoided using the notion of "race" in examining social relations in the Los Angeles metroplex. In a study of ethnic tension in a suburban community, Ngin made clear that tensions between the native multiethnic residents and the new Asian immigrants over public school resources were grounded in notions of "belonging" and "imagined community" rather than ideas that emphasized differences between "races," "ethnicities," or "cultures," as implied by a term such as "white-Asian relationship."

Racialization from Within

While immigrant groups are racialized by the dominant group, they are simultaneously engaged in defining and redefining their group identity. In this process of self-definition, immigrant groups are connected by their language and cultural, religious, and political orientation, or other factors influencing affiliation. Although it may be claimed that ethnicity is a subjective, constructed concept and cannot be defined objectively by means of social cultural indicators (e.g., those with the same language and cultural characteristics may not consider themselves one community), subjective ethnic identification can often lead to the creation of ethnic institutions such as newspapers and schools, in order to express that sense of "peoplehood." Thus, Asians and Latinos have created separate ethnic, cultural, political, and economic organizations to meet their needs in an increasingly diverse society. These institutions and structures provide autonomous networks separate from conventional institutions of the dominant culture. The point may be made, though, that these "networks" do not exist outside the political economy and class structure of society.

Examples of some of these Asian groups include Chinese-language schools, Korean churches, and the Chinese Lions Club in areas with a critical mass of Chinese or Korean residents. These affiliations are based on the members' linguistic and cultural similarity, and are no different from early Italian American and Polish American ethnic organizations. These ethnic activities are consistent with the traditional definition of ethnicity, where the emphasis is on a socially defined sense of "peoplehood" based generally on concepts of shared culture and common origin. In California, this "ethnicity-in-itself" is created in part by ethnic enclaves, which serve as buffers between the different groups and the dominant population. These ethnic organizations are extremely diverse, even within the same subethnic and/or linguistic group. As an example, Chinese "ethnic" organizations in Los Angeles may include groups based on regional or dialect origin (Canton Association, Hakka Association, and Fukien Association); lineage or surname (Wong Family Benevolent Association of Los Angeles); trade or guild (Chinese Produce Merchants Association, Chinese Chamber of Commerce, United Chinese Restaurant Association, and Chinese Cooks' Training School); religion (Chinese United Methodist Church, First Chinese Baptist Church, and Southern California Chinese Buddhist Temple); and nonprofit organizations (Chinese Historical Society of Southern California, Chinese American Citizen's Alliance, and Chinatown Service Center).

This "ethnicity-in-itself" is contrasted with "ethnicity-for-itself," which includes associations with coethnic or other ethnic groups for the purpose of political empowerment and entitlement. Awareness of their common plight and similar experiences leads other groups to lend their support by emphasizing the "community of memory," defining the boundary with which they can develop their own culture and the sharing of common experience. This ethnic awareness is actively promoted to serve clearly defined social and political objectives. We regard "ethnicity-for-itself" as racialization from within. This racialization from within serves as a political defense strategy in the face of perceived and/or real adversity or disadvantage. It is this process of renegotiation and redefinition that defines the group's relationship with the dominant society.

An example of "ethnicity-for-itself" is the increasing number of Asian American and Latino organizations in Southern California. These organizations are themselves conglomerates of much smaller ethnic groups. A Los Angeles Asian American organization, the Asian American Pacific Planning Council (APPACON), for example, represents thirty-three Asian American organizations. In Orange County, *Los Amigos,* an organization comprising about two dozen Latino interest groups, meets once a month to discuss issues and problems in the Latino community. Through collective bargaining power, these groups are able to represent their diverse constituency and to exert political pressure on the local government.

The politics of "ethnicity-for-itself" can be understood in terms of Benedict Anderson's (1991) concept of "imagined community." The "ethnicity" used as a basis for organization is "imagined" because it enables potential alliances across communities of diverse national origins, cultural backgrounds, and internal hierarchies within the groups. It also allows a significant commitment to a sense of "horizontal comradeship" in the struggle for limited state resources. This "imagined community" leads us away from essentialist notions of cultural and biological bases for alliance. So it is not "race" or "ethnicity" or "culture" that constructs the grounds for these politics; rather, it is the way ethnicity is internally racialized within changing class relations to constitute group alliance. The ethnic consciousness and the politics that develops is an important line of cleavage and an important sociopolitical force shaping contemporary U.S. society.

In Los Angeles, the legacy of an institutionalized fixation on "racial" categories has obscured important political debates about the growing gap between rich and poor. For instance, the politics of "racial turf" has further compartmentalized, fragmented, and racialized public discourse. At an off-the-record dinner with Latino journalists in early April 1992, newly elected Los Angeles County Supervisor Gloria Molina was asked to comment on a reporter's contention that local African American political leaders were continuing to deny Latinos their fair share of the city's political and economic resources. Molina replied that she understood the reporter's frustration. Sooner or later, she went on, Latino leaders like her would have to persuade their African American counterparts to face up to the political consequences of demographic reality. Latinos are ready to accept the rewards of being the county's new majority. Latino leaders insist that because their constituencies have grown in numbers, they deserve a proportionate share of the region's economic wealth. African American leaders, by contrast, argue that their constituencies are entitled to a larger share of economic resources to compensate for past injuries and ongoing exclusions.

Founded on this image is what we term the "zero-sum picture" of "race relations." Racialized groups in Los Angeles are considered to be deeply at odds with one another, their members "naturally separate" and antagonistic toward one another. Benefits to the one are perceived as costs to the other. In a *Los Angeles Times* poll (Merl 1997), two-thirds of the respondents indicated that "race relations" in Los Angeles were poor, and 39 percent said that they had seen no change since the riot of 1992.[9]

The racialization of ethnic groups and the dialectical process of resistance through racialization from within underscore the social construction of the idea of "race" and "ethnicity." The careful delineation of the metamorphosis of these ideas is important in that it enables us to refute the biological concept of "race" and to recognize the self-racialization of ethnic groups.

An Ethnicity Paradigm

In the 1960s, individuals rooted in an emancipatory agenda of Asian American and Chicano/Latino communities wrote much of the scholarly literature on Asian Americans and Latinos. Along with African American, Native American, and women's studies, these were political projects whose writings were deeply rooted in the origin of the discipline. Both Asian American and Chicano are notions constructed for the purpose of political alignment, empowerment, and opposition to the dominant racialized discourse. The result was that internal divisions among Asian Americans and Chicanos were veiled, thereby privileging the politically united front in the struggle against "white" domination. Sometimes this front aligned with, and sometimes differed from, black studies (Wong 1995).

Nevertheless, the notion of "people of color" provided an instant cross-group solidarity. This ethnicity paradigm, however, has also focused on a division between Asian and Asian American studies and between Latin American and Chicano/Latino studies even as the boundaries between the two began to blur (Wong 1995, 5). Asian studies and Latin American studies emerged as area studies during the Cold War era to serve U.S. global interests. Asian American studies and Chicano studies, as mentioned earlier, arose out of student awareness of their position within the larger social and political complexes during the civil rights and antiwar movements of the 1960s.

In recent years, a unique combination of economic, political, and social influences in the world and in the United States have made theorizing about Asian American and Latino populations in Southern California more complex than before. Instead of focusing solely on the concerns of the Asians and Latinos in California, scholars need to take into account the transnational and diasporic nature of their experience.[10] Unlike the earlier migrants who were unable to visit their homeland frequently, if ever, modern-day Chinese migrants, for instance, are connected to their homeland both in China and in historical settlements in Thailand, Singapore, Manila, and Calcutta (Pan 1990). Others are connected to their kin in global urban centers not only by their common culture and involvement in trade but also by contacts through modern technology, such as air travel, fax, and the Internet.

However, this transnational and diasporic reality among Asian Americans and Latinos is often obscured by the need for solidarity among minorities in the United States in their struggle and resistance to racism by the dominant society, as mentioned earlier. The result is that the foci of Asian American studies and Chicano/Latino studies have remained locked into a "race-ethnic" paradigm.

Culture, Globalization, and the Political Economy of the Metropolis

As the United States orients itself toward the "Pacific Century" (Borthwick 1992) and as countries in North America become one economic unit through the implementation of the North American Free Trade Agreement (NAFTA), new questions need to be raised about the current analytical models that examine identity formation, cultural orientation, and socioeconomic classes among new Asian and Latino immigrants. Emerging from the recognition of this transnational and global concern, diaspora studies have been offered as an alternative model for examining Asian Americans. Thus, as argued eloquently by Wong (1995) about the new immigrants, "instead of being mere suppliants at the 'golden door,' desperate to trade their sense of ethnic identity for a share of American plenty, many of today's Asian immigrants regard the U.S. as simply one of many possible places to exercise their portable capital and portable skills" (5). The limited material success of middle-class immigrant populations should be attributed, in part, to their professional training received abroad and to the capital they brought with them and not to some inherent cultural entrepreneurial essentialism, as argued by the new cultural determinists (Kotkin 1992).

Some of these transnational ties date back to the end of the sixteenth century, connecting trade and labor migration between Latin America and Asia in a geographic and political "Spanish-Pacific" network (Hu-DeHart 1994). In the mid-nineteenth century, large numbers of Chinese and East Indian coolie laborers worked in the sugar plantation and mining industries (251–78). Cultural influence was evident in the popular *china poblana,* an embroidered blouse worn by Mexican women in central Mexico (252), and in the numerous and popular *chifas,* or Chinese restaurants, in Lima and other Peruvian towns (271).

Five hundred years later, this "Spanish-Pacific" connection is manifested in expected ways: Spanish-speaking retailers in the Los Angeles garment district are often ethnic Chinese and Koreans from Peru and other Latin American countries who have established their businesses in the section dominated by other immigrants. Like other Chinese and Korean merchants in Los Angeles, these retailers also hire local Latinas as sales clerks in the garment district, as in the example of Young Suk Lee, the Los Angeles fashion retailer mentioned at the beginning of this chapter. Other examples of the juxtaposition of peoples and cultures in the global economy include the branches of Asian-owned businesses in Mexico headquartered in Monterey Park, a suburban city near Los Angeles, commonly referred to as "Little Taipei" by the Chinese population.

The East Asian multinationals, as global companies, defy categorization as to their national origin and loyalty. Hitachi Consumer Products of America, for instance, is headquartered in Orange County, California, with a *maquiladora* branch (Hitachi Consumer Products de Mexico) in Tijuana along the Mexican border. It employs workers from both Orange County, California, and Tijuana, Mexico, and operates other branches in Asia and the rest of the world (Crouch 1992, 1, 28, 30).

The migration of labor as a result of the internationalization of companies is a relatively new area of research (Barnet and Cavanagh 1994; Greider 1997). In the migration of labor between north and south, it is not surprising that Hu-DeHart cautions, "any current and future conceptualization of Latin America must contend with the El Norte phenomenon and integrate at least Mexico, if not the rest of the Pacific Rim of Latin America, into its configuration" (cited in Barnet and Cavanagh 1994, 271). Therefore, the local, regional, and ethnic economy and community cannot be understood without understanding the global connections of these companies and the flow of labor and capital.

In Chicano cultural studies, the notion of *La Frontera* and the recognition of the porosity of the borders is a long-standing tradition. Indeed, Renato Rosaldo, in *Culture and Truth: The Remaking of Social Analysis* (1989), coined the term "borderland" for social analysis. Chicana feminist scholars have done some of the most ambitious and critical theorizing on the concept of *La Frontera* (Saldivar-Hull 2000). Awareness of the connections between people, capital, and globalization has produced significant research on the subject even though these have not been the dominant interest within ethnic studies (Glick Schiller, Basch, and Blanc 1994; King 1997; Ong and Nonini 1997). A study particularly worth citing is Thann-dam Truong's *Sex, Money and Morality: Prostitution and Tourism in Southeast Asia* (1990), which implicates the international tourist industry in the migration of women from Southeast Asia. Equally significant is the collection of papers edited by Kathryn Ward (1990) that examines women workers within the context of global restructuring.

In this transitional community, individual orientation is based on distant transnational and diasporic concerns, thereby blurring the boundaries between the two homelands. The homeland of one's birth, ancestry, and culture and the new homeland of one's livelihood and possible future are intertwined. Yet in the language of the everyday person in the Southland, these complex issues and emotions are expressed as "immigrants want to keep their culture" and "immigrants do not view assimilation in the same way as immigrants of the past." These mostly "American-centered" foci are unable to capture the changing meaning of identity and ethnicity among transnational and diasporic Asian Americans and Latinos.

These sentiments regarding the immigrants' mostly transnational and diasporic concerns and ties have led many in the local community to question their commitment to the community, their political allegiance, and their alliances, both old and new. As a result, Latinos and Asian Americans have become the objects of an emerging wave of anti-immigrant measures.

Contemporary Racisms

How are contemporary groups racialized? And how might we understand contemporary racism? In the racism of the past, physical features, morals, and cultural characteristics were used to target individual ethnic groups for racist actions, laws, and policies. In contemporary racism, most legal discriminations occur less often, and fewer phenotypical characteristics are employed in the discourse of the immigrant groups in formal legislative policies. Increasingly, opposition to immigrant groups receiving services is framed in the language of reverse discrimination, as seen in the successful effort mounted by the University of California Board of Regents to dismantle affirmative action policies in regard to university admissions and the employment of minorities and women. The other form of opposition has been in the creation of policies and legislation targeting immigrants. The welfare reform bill, for instance, was designed to ban noncitizens and immigrants from welfare and public assistance programs. Asian Americans and Latinos are the groups most severely affected because of their immigration status. Therefore, antipathy against racialized groups in California should be viewed in the larger political and economic context. These responses cannot be explained solely as the product of "racial" animus.

In contemporary U.S. society, the stimuli that led to the renewed attack on Latino immigrants can be attributed, first, to the political posturing of politicians during election years. Negative imagery of immigrants as welfare dependents draining the economy is articulated by both the U.S.-born population and the politicians and is often politically legitimized by the state and by popular media. Second, acts of violence and discrimination against racialized populations can be understood as attempts to define the local imagined "community" alluded to earlier (Anderson 1991; Miles and Phizacklea 1981; Ngin 1995).

The local American imagined community, a community based on the ethos of biblical foundation, republicanism, and individualism, is unable to envision those with different values as being part of the same community (Bellah et al. 1985). Asian Americans and Latinos continue to be racialized as the "Other." Thus, in another study conducted by Ngin (1996) on Asian youth, for example, the targeting of Asian youth as gang members by police officers and school board members was based on a parochial idea of Asian culture, one drawn from a simplistic understanding of Buddhism and Daoism rather than one based on what Americanized Asian youths actually do. In this case, it was a process of racialization—the representation process of another—that led to the exclusion and victimization of legitimate members of the county's citizenry.

For the most part, racism today need not invoke "race" as a criterion to extol superiority. Lawsuit charges of racial discrimination are often based on allegations of exclusion or unequal treatment toward certain minority groups rather than on the inferiority of their "race." For instance, United Parcel Service of America, Inc. (UPS) was named in a lawsuit which alleged that the parcel carrier discriminates against its black employees in Oakland, California. In their filing of the lawsuit, UPS employees claimed that the company "reserves the most desirable and promotable work assignments and positions—and the training necessary to achieve them and to advance them within the company—for its non-African-American employees" ("Lawsuit Charges UPS Discriminates" 1997).

Indeed, the shift from "race" to racialization highlights and emphasizes the constant process of social construction and reconstruction of the "Other" (through a process of signification and representation) and the Self (through racialization from within). This process of attributing meaning to the use of "race" in different contexts is used as a category of inclusion, as a category of resistance, and as a category of exclusion. As a category of inclusion, a people are represented and conceptualized as members of one's group. As a category of resistance, the conceptualization and reconceptualization of the Self is an attempt to unify ethnic groups of diverse origin, to set up new models of social relations, and to empower a community based on the notion of "race" or ethnicity or culture (Le-Espiritu 1992; Muñoz 1989; White 1990). As a category of exclusion, the idea of "race" has long been employed to justify and legitimate colonial expansion, slavery, and discrimination. In the United States, the 1790 Act specifically prohibited "nonwhites" from becoming citizens.

Subsequent enactments of other legal decisions (the 1882 Chinese Exclusion Act, the 1920 Alien Land Law, the 1923 *Thind* decision, and the 1922 *Ozawa* case, inter alia) were similarly based on the idea of "race" to exclude categories of people deemed unfit by the larger polity or culture. The complex relationships of exploitation and resistance, grounded in differences of class and ethnicity, give rise to a multiplicity of ideological constructions of the racialized "Other." The analytical task of understanding racism today must therefore describe in detail the "racist" events themselves and the community's interpretations of these events (Hatcher and Troyna 1993, 2; Ngin 1996, 94). Unfortunately, most college textbooks continue to refer to racism as a belief in the existence of biologically distinct groups that are hierarchically ranked. A group's physical characteristics are linked to some psychological or intellectual capacity that is used to distinguish between superior and inferior groupings. Recent books on racism also continue to emphasize the language of race to understand discrimination and exclusion. According to Carl Rowan, one of America's most distinguished journalists, racism in the United States today is seen as based on the resurgence of these old ideas in nineteenth-century biology. He cites, for example, the Freeman militia, a small Montana cult, whose leaders preached that "descendants of northern Europeans are 'God's chosen people' that Jews are 'the children of Satan,' and that African Americans and other people of color are by nature dumb and immoral" (Rowan 1996, 4). Racism is, for the most part, perpetrated by members of "the Aryan nation, the skinheads, the Ku Klux Klan, and assorted militants piling up arms for what they say is a coming race war in America" (ibid., 4).

The common assertion that racism is associated with "white people" has a history of intellectual development. The term "racism" first appeared in the English language in the 1930s. It can be traced to the use of the idea of "race" by Hitler's German Nazi Party to justify the Jews as an alien and inferior "race." This painful recognition of what had been inflicted in the name of "race" (Kuhl 1994; Miles 1989, 1993) and the subsequent critical appraisal of this discourse on "race" (Benedict 1983; Montagu 1974) led to the scientific community's repudiation of this "scientific racism" (Barkan 1992). Within the United States, the resistance to racism after World War II has led to an important transformation of the term "racism."[11] Racism was redefined to argue that racism was a "white ideology" constructed to exploit African Americans and other minority groups through a complex of legal exclusion and social segregation and sustained by the construction of a representational image based on "race" and skin color. "White people" are supposed to be afflicted with the disease in the form of deeply ingrained, often unconscious, attitudes. The antidote of racism is merely a matter of changing "white" attitudes and behavior toward members of the "minority races" (Katz 1978).

The projects of the antiracist movement—the civil rights movement's *Brown v. Board of Education* case and the Civil Rights Acts of 1964 and 1965—were aimed at countering the long-standing racism targeting the minority population. These projects, while noble in intent, have been subverted and manipulated by the far right through a decontextualization and a delinking of the language of civil rights to serve a conservative agenda. The California Civil Rights Initiative—to reverse affirmative action—is a prime example of how the term "civil rights" has come to mean the opposite of what was intended in the 1960s.

What is most needed, we believe, is a refutation of the concept of "race" in order to explicitly delineate the practices of racism. Reference to the concept of "race," while stripped of its biological sense, continues to be employed in the United States in the social sense. Most people attach significance to the concept of "race" and consider it real and important in the division of humanity. As previously discussed, the categorization of populations by the U.S. Census Bureau is a profound example of this racializing project (Goldberg 1995). The reification of "race" and the employment of "race" for social analysis continue to be the norm in most social science research. If the idea of "race" has been proven false by the weight of scientific evidence, why has it maintained its centrality in cultural discourse? If social conflicts are often based on competition for scarce resources in a changing global economy and not based on differences between "races," "ethnicities," or "cultures," what justification is there to continue to use the idea of "race"? What data might be unveiled if a research focus on social relationships and conflicts were based on a model of racialization—a representation process of signification based on phenotypical and increasingly on cultural characteristics?

These signified characteristics, whether real or imaginary, are used for the purpose of inferiorization, labor exploitation, and exclusion (Balibar and Wallerstein 1991). It is possible that inferiorization, exploitation, and exclusionary measures based on racialized logic would constitute multiple kinds of racism. Therefore, we could speak of multiple forms of racism or racisms rather than a singular racism. These various forms of racism are especially virulent during election years and during temporary downturns in the economic cycle.

Indeed, a collection of essays attempting to solve the conundrum of racism has rectified the widespread presumption that racism is a monolithic phenomenon based on a set of irrational prejudices. Racism is revealed to have taken on "the mantle of scientific theory, philosophical rationality, and 'morality'" through the expression of these concerns in racist terms. Further, a major historical shift is the contemporary expression of racism in nationalist terms. Racism is now "expressed increasingly in terms of isolationist national self-image; of cultural differentiation tied to custom, tradition, and heritage; and of exclusionary immigration policies, anti-immigrant practices and criminality" (Goldberg 1990, xiv).

Forging a New Understanding

In applying Miles's argument, we reject the use of "race" and "ethnicity" as analytical categories and the framing of social relations between groups as "race relations." As discussed earlier in this volume, we find that the traditional "race relations" approach grounded in the black-white paradigm is incapable of providing insights into the complex nature of multiple racisms in an increasingly diverse society. We referred to the instances of racialization of Asian and Latino/Chicano populations as those social processes whereby social groups are singled out for unequal treatment on the social significance of physical or genetic differences. The significance of this theoretical approach is its application to the examination of social groups other than black and white populations. Furthermore, the process of racialization should be equally applicable in the examination of racialization within and between groups.

We have also noted the process of "racialization from within" for the purpose of in-group solidarity and alliance. This distinction provides an analytical framework for understanding the dynamics of ethnic politics and multiple cultural identities within the context of a changing political economy. While not positing an economically reductionist argument, we do maintain that we live under capitalist relations with class and racialized inequalities. Furthermore, this critique of capitalism is more timely and necessary than ever before.

Clearly, there are major areas where further research and theorizing are needed to move us toward a new understanding of both the expression and consequences of racisms. First, we need comparative studies of racialized groups in the United States. As suggested, this will require a radical break with the dominant "race relations" paradigm that assigns analytical status to the idea of "race" and frames "racial matters" in black-and-white terms. Second, an expanded research agenda is required to address with analytical specificity the nature and meaning of class relations within racialized populations and communities, to examine how these changing class formations manifest themselves in community politics and state intervention. While different racisms have been hegemonic, they have always been challenged and resisted. Studies of resistance must be undertaken, in particular, to demonstrate the complexities and contradictions within the social, cultural, political, and economic terrain that arise from the struggles against racisms.

Finally, in this era of capitalist restructuring, an exploration of the changing nature of citizenship must be undertaken with specificity and rigor. This project will be made more rewarding through a creative class-based notion of citizenship linking the "cultural" with the "public."

We recognize that the materiality of contemporary capitalism with its structural inequalities of income and power is a central feature of contemporary U.S. society and that our quest for a more democratic notion of citizenship in a changing political economy must advance and articulate a compelling vision of social and economic democracy. In effect, we are seeking a set of theoretical foundations for a renewed Marxian political economy that will support the reinvigoration of an antiracist struggle, anchored in the renewal of a class politics for the twenty-first century.

3

Language Rights and
the Empire of Capital

Ultimately language politics are determined by material interests—
that is, struggles for social and economic supremacy, which nor-
mally lurk beneath the surface of the public debate. (Crawford
2000, 10)

Every relationship of "hegemony" . . . occurs not only within a nation, between the various forces of which the nation is composed,
but in the international and world-wide field, between complexes of
national and continental civilizations. (Gramsci 1971, 350)

Empires do not emerge naturally and innocently. . . . They are
welded together with deliberate deceit, greed and ruthless violence.
(Parenti 1995, 23)

In 1996, Congress ratified a bill that designated English the
federal government's official language of business. This was the first time
in U.S. history that any form of official federal language policy had been
instituted. Coincidentally, it was during the same year that the campaign
for Proposition 227 was initiated, which ushered in the gradual but
steady demise of bilingual education in California. Since *Lau v.
Nichols*,[1] bilingual education in California had enjoyed some legitimacy
and attention within official educational public policy arenas. Proposition 227 systematically stripped away the ability of bilingual communities in California to claim bilingual instruction as an educational right
protected by legislation—a right so painfully earned during the civil
rights era. As a consequence, Latino and other minority-language students find themselves immersed in English-only classes, while bilingual-
education advocates struggle to retain a limited foothold on bilingual ed-

ucation in public schools today. Accordingly, few formal public venues are now left to address questions of bilingual education in any consistent and rigorous manner, as the steady demise of bilingual education is now seen by many as a fait accompli.

In many ways, the success of Proposition 227 in California (and in its revised formulation in states such as Massachusetts and Arizona) represents but the tip of the iceberg in neoliberal efforts to "turn back the clock" on cultural and linguistic rights,[2] not only in this country but also around the globe. Hence, we argue that the decline of bilingual-education rights in the United States must be understood in relation to a long-standing history of international struggles for the cultural and linguistic rights of oppressed populations around the world.

We can trace the racialization of language to the political practices of the ancient Greeks, who ranked a population's capacity for civilization according to the language they spoke (Fredrikson 2002). "Barbarian" was the classification of the time—a racialized term used to discriminate by language rather than phenotypic traits. And in ancient Greece, as in the politics of the modern nation-state, language represented a significant social index in the determination of eligibility to citizenship rights.

Today more than ever, the struggle for linguistic rights must be linked to the racialized constructions of the modern nation-state,[3] with its penchant for unbridled economic colonialism and capitalist-imperialist expansion—now expressed by many scholars with the euphemistic term "globalization." Wood (2003) provides the more useful analytical term "empire of capital" to refer to a new form of imperialism that is reshaping the world today. The political economy of the new imperialism influences in a variety of ways the material conditions of both native bilingual populations and language-minority immigrants.

Many immigrants in the United States, for example, have been forced to flee their countries as a direct outcome of regional wars and economic impoverishment—conditions created by contemporary U.S. foreign economic policies. U.S. foreign trade agreements, such as the General Agreement on Tariffs and Trade (GATT) and the North American Free Trade Agreement (NAFTA),[4] have generated a decline in living standards both in this country and abroad. In the eight years since the initiation of NAFTA, almost 800,000 jobs have disappeared, as factories have closed down and exported jobs to cheap-labor-market regions such as Mexico, Taiwan, and the Caribbean. But instead of raising the quality of life for foreign workers, NAFTA lowered it (Lugo 2004; Gonzalez 2000; Parenti

1995). As a result of the deleterious conditions created by globalization, many immigrants seeking economic opportunities ventured to the United States. The outcome of the current geopolitical economic crisis in Latin America has been particularly visible in California, which has historically served as a port of entry for many Spanish-speaking immigrants.

Nearly 50 percent of the 40 million Latinos residing in California today are foreign born. In Los Angeles County alone, more than 4.2 million residents are Latino. And although the largest percentage is from Mexico, there is a growing number of immigrants from other Latin American countries, including El Salvador, Nicaragua, and Argentina. Population projections estimate that by the year 2005 "minority" residents will become the majority of the population in most large urban centers, which is already the case in many large U.S. cities today. Further, the 2000 census documented an astonishing increase in Latino immigrants in the Deep South, showing Latino population increases of nearly 300 percent in North Carolina, Arkansas, Georgia, and Tennessee.

This growing number of diverse Spanish-speaking immigrants poses important questions regarding how the nation-state will contend with complex issues, which are bound to require the redefining of current ideas of citizenship. These changes and the implications they hold for the future are generating much interest in notions of cultural citizenship and transcitizenship (Mirón and Inda 2004), political concepts that seek to challenge nativist views about bilingual education and other racialized language policies around the globe.[5]

There is no doubt that a legacy of racialized language policies has resulted in a long history of language struggles in Europe, Latin America, Africa, Australia, New Zealand, and other parts of the world. The common practice of modern nation-states to blatantly racialize language-minority populations within their own borders persists even today—particularly when the dominant class judges such actions to be in the interest of national security or economic well-being. More often than not, the move to obtain cultural and class dominion over a nation's residents has rendered minority-language speakers problematic to capitalist accumulation. To ensure that the "Other" is kept in line with the system of production, racialized institutional policies and practices have led to widespread deportation, assimilation, incarceration, or extermination of minority populations.

British historian Michael Wood (2002) estimates that during the period of colonial expansion in the sixteenth century "several tens of millions" of indigenous people in the Western hemisphere were victims of disease, warfare, and famine at the hands of European conquistadors (17). "By the late 1500s, a mere century after the conquest began, scarcely two million natives remained in the entire hemisphere. An average of more than one million people perished annually for most of the sixteenth century, in what has been called 'the greatest genocide in human history'" (Gonzalez 2000, 10). In the twentieth century, millions of deaths related to systematic genocide of populations, or what Samantha Powers (2002) terms "race murders," have been recorded. Beyond the most often remembered—the death of six million Jews at the hands of the Third Reich—there are the mass deaths of the Kurds in Turkey and Iraq and the Tutsi in Rwanda, the killing fields of the Khmer Rouge in Cambodia, and the ethnic cleansings in Bosnia and Kosovo.

Currently, repressive political forces are at work in Spain, where Moroccan immigrants are routinely stopped and searched, while educators debate furiously regarding the drain that immigrant children are having on educational resources because of their lack of Spanish skills. Similar conditions exist for working-class immigrant populations in Germany, Switzerland, and England. Kurd and Roma (or "Gypsy," as they are often called) immigrants have been racialized in every country they have attempted to settle.

Native-born bilingual populations rendered "Other" within their own lands have experienced a fate similar to that of racialized immigrant groups. In Spain, the elite-language campaign of *armas y letras* in the fifteenth century and the Church-inspired *sangre pura* ideology (Fredrikson 2002) still casts a shadow on the political imagination. To this date, social struggles tied to questions of cultural and linguistic determination persist. For example, conflicts are still common between the Madrileños, who represent the mainstream, and the Basques, Gallegos, and Catalans, who have often been relegated to the margins of Spain's political and economic life.

In even more intense ways, this phenomenon is at work in the lives of many existing indigenous populations of Africa, Australia, Latin America, and the United States. For example, in Australia and New Zealand, both Aboriginal and Maori communities persist in their struggles to retain language rights. In the United States, the geopolitics of native Hawaiians and other indigenous peoples encompass ardent efforts to keep both their language and culture from becoming extinct. But these are examples of language communities that have managed to survive; most have not.

The world's languages are dying off at an alarming rate. Of the estimated six thousand languages in the world, more than half are expected to become extinct by the end of the century, with only 10 percent considered to have a secure future. In today's global village, only one hundred languages are spoken by 90 percent of the world's population (Nettle and Romaine 2000). Tove Skutnabb-Kangas (2000), a leading international biodiversity and linguistic-rights advocate, argues that the majority of language communities over the last hundred years have become victims of linguistic genocide—that is, the language is killed rather than the people. She explains this genocide as a desire to destroy potential competition for political and economic power in order to eliminate any claims to nation-state rights among indigenous and minority populations. In this light, we can better understand linguistic genocide in the plight of African Americans who were separated from their families and forced into slave labor; the Native American Indians who were stripped of much of their land and had their children arbitrarily removed to English-speaking boarding schools; and Mexican, Puerto Rican, and Chinese workers who were exploited for cheap labor and subjected to substandard housing and education.

Given the pressure and strain to survive such conditions, many have lost their linguistic connection to their ancestral culture. Again, key to this discussion is the manner in which racism, manifested through processes of linguistic racialization, is intricately linked to political-economic power, control of natural resources, and the subordination of those inferiorized as the "Other." Balibar and Wallerstein's (1991) notion of inferiorization, which defines modern conditions of racism in which labor rights are denied and immigrant workers are forced into menial jobs and low-level positions, is once again useful in framing our discussion.

Moreover, Balibar's (2003) recent work on the notion of "election/selection" is helpful in understanding the ideological justifications of empire building that have often accompanied cultural and linguistic suppression of populations. He suggests that the historical notion of "election" to rule is used to substantiate the right to govern over lesser beings and "select" (or dispense), in the name of the nation-state, those populations considered a potential threat to the state's welfare.

Underpinning much of this discourse are unexamined assumptions of the "Other." Many of these assumptions seem closely tied to religious influences such as the biblical story of the Tower of Babel, in which linguistic differences are said to be the result of God's punishment of humanity (Nettle and Romaine 2000). Such an influence could easily be used to justify early "scientific" beliefs among anthropologists who predicted that the language of "savages" would surely amalgamate, until one day there would exist but one superior language spoken by all on the planet. Indeed, resonating here is Darwin's central thesis: the survival of the fittest. According to Balibar (2003), these attitudes are also inscribed with the belief that human civilization is expected to strive for transcendence of a "divine" humanity over a "hellish animalism." Hence, it is not surprising that the "othering" of cultures and languages outside the mainstream has consistently burdened minority-language populations with proving themselves to be "decent human beings," worthy of entrance into the inner sanctum of nation-state citizenship.

In exclusionary public-policy discourse, it is not unusual to find derogatory animalistic reference made to the intellectual, linguistic, phenotypic, sexual, or criminal tendencies of subordinate groups. In *Documents of American Prejudice*, Joshi (1999) compiled a series of official historical documents that testify to the validity of this claim. One such example is found in the document by John Box, a minister and longtime U.S. representative from Texas, who addressed Congress on February 9, 1928, to support the need for strong immigration laws (Congressional Record 69, No. 3). He argued passionately that

> [the] purpose of the immigration law is the protection of American racial stock from further degradation or change through mongrelization. The Mexican . . . is a mixture of Mediterranean-blooded Spanish peasant with low-grade Indians who did not fight to extinction but submitted, and multiplied as serfs. This blend of low-grade Spaniard, peonized Indian, and Negro slave mixes with Negroes, mulatoes [*sic*], and other mongrels, and some sorry whites, already here. The prevention of such mongrelization and the degradation it causes is one of the purposes of our laws which the admission of these people will tend to defeat. Every incoming race causes blood mixture, but if this were not true, a mixture of blocs of peoples of different races has a bad effect upon citizenship, creating more race conflicts and weakening national character (cited in Joshi 1999, 481–82).

Unfortunately, current media debates on the problem of immigration are no less racializing, except for twenty-first-century political speak which obfuscates racialized class sentiments. Newspaper, television, and film portrayals of immigrants fulfill their hegemonic role of racialization by presenting immigrant populations as uncivilized, ignorant, or dangerous. Such distortions are fueled by moral panic and act upon consumers of media in a multitude of ways, but principally they call into question the culturally democratic policies in U.S. society. Deep hostilities toward immigrant populations expressed by nativists and neoliberal conservatives raise serious concerns regarding the future of language rights in this country.

Sassen (1998) concludes, "Immigration policy continues to be characterized by its formal isolation from major processes, as if it were possible to handle migration as a bounded, closed event. There are, one could say, two major epistemic communities—one concerning the flow of capital and information; the other, immigration" (62). We argue that in the United States a tremendous rift exists between, on the one hand, the nation-state's advocacy for the open and unrestricted movement of commerce, trade, finance capital, technology, and ideas, and on the other hand, the deeply isolationist polices to restrict the movement of people and workers across its borders. The tragedy of September 11[6] has been capitalized on to join the efforts of Homeland Security with existing Immigration and Naturalization Service (INS) activities in the careful regulation and monitoring of the movement of people. The conflicting and contradictory nature of these national objectives has served to intensify the anti-immigrant debate and the subsequent racialization that results in cultural and linguistic domination of populations. It is significant to consider this point in light of the fact that California, where the contemporary suppression of bilingual education in schools began, is also the fifth-largest economy in the world. Hence, the post–civil rights era has been supplanted by the global era, in which both surveillance and neoliberal excess are welcomed and normalized.

However, long before September 11, the political rhetoric that contributed to the passage of Proposition 227 in California was well underway.

In the mid-eighties Ernest L. Boyer, president for the Carnegie Foundation for the Advancement of Teaching, appealed to American public opinion to once again rethink its stance on allowing non-English-speaking foreigners to immigrate into the United States. He noted that the national community's social tensions were now signified by bilingual education—a code word, he argued, that had turned the schools into "the battle ground" of the nation. (Oboler 1995, 29)

Though the process of contact and exchange has obviously altered expressions of racism, Boyer's words still echo old notions that deem cultural and linguistic differences a fundamental threat to the very stability and unity of this country. Iris Zavala (1992) suggests that the reason for this perception of threat is the central role that language and culture play in the conservation of the nation-state: language and culture are used within the dominant society to create an illusion of cohesion or the appearance of stability in a world always in flux. Efforts to fortify this illusion of stability are heavily intensified during historical periods of political economic crisis and military expansionism. Both of these conditions have steadily increased in the last two decades, with massive layoffs of workers across the country and increasing military action overseas.

As job opportunities decline, the policing of the barrios, anti-immigrant sentiments, and English-only efforts intensify,[7] thus tightening the very controls that were loosened at an earlier time, when the need for cheap, unskilled labor existed. This intensification is fueled by the arguments of conservative political gatekeepers who allege that undocumented immigrants take away jobs from citizens, lower property values, threaten law and order, consume education and welfare resources, and now constitute a national security risk. Many of these disingenuous public debates center on the need for tighter patrol of the U.S.-Mexico border, while seldom mentioned is the U.S.-Canada border, which is far more accessible to anyone wishing to cross illegally.

Current anti-immigrant sentiments and efforts to thwart bilingualism are every bit as politically vicious as they were in the early decades of the twentieth century—fueled by similar political alliances and by the xenophobic nativist rhetoric of conservative policy makers and big business. Parallel conditions of these historical eras include increasing immigration, burgeoning student enrollment in urban centers, economic decline, and copious military spending overseas.

Assimilative policies and practices developed in the early 1900s continue to shape the hidden barriers that stall the implementation of linguistic educational reform today. However, differences in the impact of these policies across various immigrant groups may be best explained as a disparity in the racialization process experienced by European versus non-European immigrants. Therefore, despite the initial experiences of racialization suffered by Irish, Italian, Polish, and Russian immigrants, it was always presumed that these European immigrants could be absorbed into the cultural definition of the American nation-state. No such presumption was made of non-European populations. Joseph Check (2002) describes the differences:

> Racial "indigestion" caused by European immigrants arriving faster than they could be absorbed may have been unpleasant, but at least it presumed that in time, through schooling, they could be absorbed and the dilution on "our national stock" reversed. This presumption rested, in turn, on an implied kinship between all Europeans, whether "noble" Anglo-Saxons or "degenerate" Irish, Italians, Poles, or Russians. No such kinship was presumed to exist with non-Europeans groups: Native Americans, Asians, Puerto Ricans, and African-Americans. There was no argument for assimilation-through-education, and so widespread exclusion from mainstream activities (including education) or relegation to second-class status was a common practice for these groups (50).

Check's work raises the idea of kinship and its relationship to linguistic preservation. The use of a shared language (or dialect) is one way in which a sense of kinship is constituted and participation in communal life guaranteed. Kinship here includes cultural processes that make social relations meaningful, including forms of address, modes of reckoning, and story telling (Amariglio, Resnick, and Wolff 1988). Through linguistic practices, kin subjects are produced or incorporated as members of a collective subjectivity, while providing them with a sense of identity.

In cases of cultural subordination, contact with school power and authority is used to erode cultural values and practices, resulting in generational alteration in the practices and collective life of the group. One of the tactics employed by the dominant society in transforming and administering diverse communities of working-class immigrant populations is to restrict their movement within society and access to opportunities. The key here is to create conditions by which communal surplus labor (or participation) can be redistributed, and to outlaw or obstruct participation away from communally shared rituals and practices designed to reinforce and reproduce the original kinship structures (Amariglio, Resnick, and Wolff 1988)—redirecting identity, participation, and loyalty to the state.

Institutional efforts to obstruct minority-language development and its uses, as well as efforts to curtail rituals or cultural practices, are all implicated here.[8] Again, such practices tend to become most severe during times of imperial expansion and economic decline, when the "other" language and culture is determined to be a detriment to national unity and the process of capital accumulation. Over time, institutional assimilative practices and policies, tied to the restriction of both education and the labor market, function to normalize the loss of primary culture and language among immigrant and indigenous populations. And as Nettle and Romaine (2000) argue:

> The radical restructuring of human societies, which has led to the dominance of English and a few other world languages is not a case of "survival of the fittest," not the outcome of competition or free choice among equals in an idealized market place. It is instead the result of unequal social change resulting in striking disparities in resources between developed and developing countries (18).

Hence, globalized manifestations of racism in the guise of language and culture subordination are intricately linked to the internationalization of capital and the consolidation of political power. Yet, despite this reality, many public advocates of bilingual education still address major problems in urban schools solely in terms of curriculum, pedagogy, bilingual teachers, instructional materials, new technology, or additional research. Although these approaches continue to be important to our work, their political power and sustenance, if achieved, must be linked to the larger structural realities and forces that shape their necessity in the first place. We are not suggesting that those pedagogical dimensions are not important to the development of bilingualism or bilingual education. Instead, we posit that the struggle for an emancipatory education in general and bilingual education in particular must be grounded in an understanding of the contemporary political economic contexts that shape the lives of bilingual students and their families, communities, and teachers.

If the bilingual education movement in this country is to have any long-term or significant impact, it must become intimately joined to an international project for social justice, human rights, and economic democracy. Our failure to make this connection weakened our political efforts in California and was partly responsible for the limited community involvement (particularly across working populations) in efforts to defeat Proposition 227 there.

Lastly, it is imperative that current bilingual-education debates move away from the single-issue approach of the past. Public policies driven by market imperatives pose serious threats to democratic institutions. For Wood (2003), the "empire of capital" spans the globe with pervasive and intrusive control over our natural resources and humanity. Thus, transcitizenship debates, anchored solidly in international antiracist and anticapitalist struggle, are essential to the struggle for language rights in these changing times.

4

Manufacturing Destinies
The Racialized Discourse
of High-Stakes Testing

Whatever its little detours may be, ultimately, *the goal of racism is dominance.* (Memmi 2000, 55)

Racialized discourse operates to construct racialized subjectivities and identities. (Gann 2000, 12)

Since its inception in the United States, the public school system has been seen as a method of disciplining children in the interest of producing a properly subordinate adult population. Sometimes conscious and explicit, and at other times a natural emanation from the conditions of dominance and subordinacy prevalent in the economic sphere, the theme of social control pervades educational thought and policy. (Bowles and Gintis 1976, 37)

In the twentieth century, public education in the United States was consistently portrayed as a liberal democratizing force, operating in the name of justice, freedom, and excellence. However, closer examination of schooling practices reveals an ideology of domination that systematically reproduces, reinforces, and sustains the hegemonic forces of social control and regulation—forces linked to class oppression, gender inequalities, and racialized exclusion. Not surprisingly, therefore, popular myths related to meritocracy, the rights and privilege of the elite, and the need for state consensus have together conserved an ideology of "race" that fuels the current craze over high-stakes testing in public schools today.

This rapidly growing phenomenon can best be understood in light of the major changes taking place in the socioeconomic landscape of U.S. society, changes that could ignite greater class conflict and social unrest than modern history has ever known. This condition continues to worsen for the growing numbers of working-class people, given recent events associated with the global political economy that have resulted in thousands of workers being laid off with fewer options for employment. Jeff Faux of the Economic Policy Institute (EPI) in Washington, D.C., echoed this theme in a 2002 speech he gave in Japan at the *Asia-Europe-U.S. Progressive Scholar's Forum: Globalization and Innovation of Politics.* In his comments, Faux confirmed that inequality has become worse. "In the short term, we can expect the U.S. unemployment rate . . . to rise" (4). "In the long term, the U.S. economy is clearly headed for a financial crisis" (8) with an account deficit of over $400 billion. Moreover, preliminary findings from *The State of Working America* (Mishel, Bernstein, and Boushey 2003) predict that unless the economy reverses course soon, working families can look forward to high and rising unemployment that will generate wage stagnation, higher poverty rates, and rising inequality. Workers' response to the impact of this economic decline on their lives is well illustrated in a recent front-page story in the *Christian Science Monitor* entitled "Labor more militant as economy teeters." The story reported, "the nation's economic slowdown is threatening millions of ordinary workers' paychecks and jobs" (Belsie 2002).

Alex Molnar (1996) in *Giving Kids the Business* points out that simultaneously with a depressed economy and worsening conditions for workers, "the rhetoric about the catastrophic failure of American public schools [has] become even more feverish" (10). Business leaders clamor for free-market solutions to educational problems, alleging that these solutions can improve education at no additional cost. These reforms conceal the fact that they "offer a public-spirited justification for introducing education to the profit motive and giving educators a healthy dose of the 'real world' in the form of competition. Most important, they keep the focus on schools and off the failure of business to promote the well-being of most of the country's citizens" (10).

In response to the pressure from business, the enterprise of education has become more and more fixated on making claims of scientific authority to carry out its instrumentalized policies in response to the academic problems faced by students from the working class and communities of color. The historical parallels between the contemporary "accountability experts" in education and the "cost-efficiency consultants" of the early part of the twentieth century are worth noting. In both historical eras there was increasing immigration, burgeoning student enrollments in urban centers, economic decline, and overt military action overseas. Moreover, big business leaders seeking to take control of public education in the early 1900s utilized the same rhetoric of corruption and the declining efficiency of public schools, so prevalent among corporate elites today, to legitimate their move. In addition,` elite businessmen ran for school boards and solicited the advice of efficiency experts like Frederick Taylor in their misguided effort to make schools function like well-oiled factory machines.

The Politics of Accountability

In today's world, corporate leaders again hold the enterprise of education hostage through their demand for new accountability measures, in exchange for support of tax hikes and budget increases. The tactics of these businessmen are closely aligned to the idea that schools should function with the efficiency of a for-profit business, with a chief executive officer (CEO) holding the reins of the district and the language and practices of schooling translated into the technical realm of accountability. These business leaders insist that measurable, scientifically based objectives should be the primary impetus for making decisions, designing curricula, and articulating the pedagogical imperatives of the classroom. They advocate fervently for an increase in standardized testing and insist, as Alex Caputo-Pearl (2001) reminds us,

> An emphasis on testing ensures that 1) schools and teachers are accountable to communities, and students are accountable for their lessons, 2) quality of education is increasing as scores increase, 3) economic and academic opportunities are expanding for students that attain higher scores, and 4) schools are accountable to a patriotic curriculum. Using standardized tests as a hammer, many of these leaders tell students to be accountable for their classwork and homework, parents to be accountable for their children's performance and teachers to be accountable for their students' performance. In doing so, they effectively marginalize discussion of the real problems in education. (4)

In the process, the yardstick of test scores has achieved an overarching prominence, seriously limiting educational debates to that of numbers and categories of students to be tested. Questions welcomed and legitimated within this narrow discourse of quality and accountability adhere to standardized testing as the most effective and legitimate means for assessing academic achievement. Rather than entertaining questions regarding student ability and overall performance, current educational debates all loop back to the issue of testing and the improvement of test scores. Thus, it is not unusual for educators to ponder questions such as: How soon can recent immigrant students be tested? What subjects and grade levels should be tested? What scores should be used to determine grade promotion or graduation? What degree of movement in the improvement of scores should be required to grant bonuses to principals? What scores should determine teacher merit pay?

With the current discourse of accountability, rarely is there any serious or substantive mention of academic success outside test score indicators. In this closed system of accountability, there is no dialogue related to the very conditions under which schooling functions, its unexamined assumptions, and its effect on students, as such questions are deemed irrelevant or scientifically irrational. Issues unrelated to the measurement of test scores are considered anecdotal at best or ideological prattle at worst, justifying their dismissal as inconsequential to public policy and educational debate.

Nowhere is this change more evident than in California, where the reform movement in support of testing and the standardization of knowledge openly and unabashedly turned the education of working-class and poor students into "drill and kill" exercises of teaching-to-the-test and highly scripted literacy instruction such as Open Court, which is being widely used by many districts. The exceedingly prescriptive nature of these practices leaves little doubt that state testing and test-driven curricula are directly or indirectly linked to an academically limiting and subordinating system of social control—one that successfully sustains the reproduction of class formation in *both* public schools and the larger society (Darder 2002).

Moreover, to ensure compliance, school funding, principal tenure, and teacher incentive pay are being determined more and more by performance contracts linked to performance as measured by a single indicator—the aggregation of student standardized test scores. Standardized testing is increasingly being used as the central mechanism for decisions about student learning, teacher and administrative practice, and overall school quality (Heubert and Hauser 1999). This is exemplified by a supplementary section published in the *Rocky Mountain News* entitled "CSAP 2002: A Guide to Results of the Students Assessment Tests." The twenty-four-page supplement (of which eighteen pages consist of test scores for Colorado schools) reported "Colorado's largest-ever release of state scores" (2E). Story headlines reveal the problems with standardized testing: "Test scores hit the wall" (2E), "Schools fare better, worse in DPS" (3E), "Affluent districts score at top" (4E), "Spotty performance to cost Jeffco $4.5 million" (4E), and "Tax dollars are tied to results in state's largest school districts" (4E).

The consequence is that the institutionalized locus of control over curriculum, teaching, and assessment, all based upon a tightly regimented set of prescriptions, not only locates authority over educational decisions at the state level but also, as mentioned earlier, gives the power over those decisions to business leaders. The insidious nature of this hegemonic mechanism of control is glaringly evident in a national commission report, issued in the early 1990s by the Ford Foundation, which estimated that nearly 130,000,000 standardized tests were being administered to elementary and secondary students, at an estimated cost of $500 million a year (Toch 1991). This has resulted in the preponderance of testing within public schools, and of the reform movement so invested in it. "Increasingly, it is in terms of standardized test scores alone that the nation judges its schools and educators judge themselves" (206).

Yet, despite its key role in the accountability reform movement, research on the use of standardized testing has found that "testing in schools historically has played an insidious role in the perpetuation of underachievement" (Darder 1991, 13), particularly among racialized, working-class students. Numerous scholars (McNeil 2000; McNeil and Valenzuela 2000; Kohn 2000; Sacks 1999; Popham 1999; Viadero 1999) question the accuracy of standardized tests and warn against the use of high-stakes testing as a single measure of progress, given their failure to measure students' abilities to judge, analyze, infer, interpret, or reason, that is, to engage in critical thought.

Standardized tests have been found even less useful in measuring the depth of students' knowledge of academic subjects. One reason for the failure of norm-referenced tests such as the Stanford 9,[1] which has been widely administered in California public schools, relates to the nature of their design. These tests are designed to rank students against one another, rather than to measure students' knowledge of the material. Many of the questions

> are intentionally developed so that a relatively high percentage of students will be tricked by them. This is an important method of differentiating one student from another in the rankings. Further, because test scores are supposed to fall into a bell curve pattern in comparing one to the other, 50% of students will always be considered "below average" or "below middle ground." (Caputo-Pearl 2001, 7)

Other reasons associated with student failure are directly tied to questions of cultural relevancy and class biases hidden in the conceptual construction and language use of standardized tests (Nieto 1996; Figueroa and Garcia 1994; Darder 1991; McNeil 1986). The construction of high-stakes tests is considered among its proponents to be a value-free scientific instrument for assessing the academic achievement of all students. However, Sonia Nieto (1996) argues that "the validity and effects of tests are questionable, particularly for children from culturally and linguistically diverse backgrounds" (91). Further, Nieto challenges testing legislation in terms of equity and diversity, concluding that instead of improving learning outcomes, it "is likely to have a negative impact . . . because gross inequities in instructional quality, resources and other support services are ignored" (91).

As if these problems were not enough, there are widespread testing problems related to the administration and scoring of tests. In New Mexico in 1992, 70 percent of superintendents reported a variety of testing errors. In Georgia, Harcourt Educational Measurement could not deliver accurate results from spring 2002's Stanford 9 tests in a timely fashion. In that same year in Nevada, officials reported that 736 sophomores and juniors had mistakenly been told they had failed the math portion of a test, although they had actually passed. And even states such as North Carolina, "considered models of accountability are struggling to come up with reliable tests" (Jonsson 2002, 11).

Even more disconcerting is the way the politics of standardized testing functions to silence and prevent greater public engagement within communities. When the only language of currency for the construction of educational policy is linked to accountability, the capacity of parents, communities, and educators to raise significant and more complex questions related to student academic success is jeopardized and impeded. Excluded are critiques based on democratic values, children's development, cultural differences, class privilege, and other critical questions that could potentially unveil the social and economic consequences of standardized testing. In the current political climate, the only conversations deemed meaningful are those directly linked to raising test scores.

In *Contradictions of School Reform: Educational Costs of Standardized Testing*, Linda McNeil (2000) sheds light on the way this insidious system of accountability is operationalized. First, the tenure for principals is replaced by "performance contracts." Their contract renewals, assignments, and annual bonuses are predicated on test score results in their schools, which reinforces the role of the principal as compliance officer and justifies the principal's intervention and control over the labor of teachers. Second, newspaper ratings and state rankings of schools disaggregate by "race" and ethnicity. All their scores must "improve."

> This disaggregating of scores gives the appearance that the system is sensitive to diversity and committed to improving minority education. This reporting, however, actually exacerbates . . . a focus on tests to the exclusion of many other forms of education. Increasingly common is the substitution of commercial test-prep materials in place of traditional curricula and instructional activities for these students. (233)

Consequently, teachers are held captive to the accountability protocol set forth by the state, with virtually no room to generate or execute more effective criteria for assessing the academic progress of their students.

The Deskilling of Teachers

The requirements for high-stakes testing of students also set into motion a series of state-mandated curricula aimed at minimizing teacher skills, in conjunction with long-term pedagogical practices of social control and regulation within schools. Increasingly, the curricula and tests are divorced from any serious consideration of critical forms of pedagogies or learning theories. The development of standardized curricula, assessment instruments, and high-stakes testing often fails to consider the wealth of research and literature on teaching and learning to inform its execution. Undoubtedly an educational system that willingly ignores curriculum theory and child development research—not to mention the social, political, and economic realities of students' lives—has the veiled organizational objective of serving as a regulatory and exclusionary mechanism to control teacher work and student outcomes.

Testing and teaching-to-the-test serve as mechanisms to instill a teacher-proof curriculum, which in many cases may include narrowly prescribed checklists for assessing minimum teaching and student skills. Undoubtedly, such regimentation makes schooling exceedingly simple for less skilled teachers. Many teachers are happy to offer routine lessons according to a standard sequence and format, preferring to function as deskilled laborers who do not have to do much thinking or preparation with respect to their practice. In contrast, a teacher-proof instructional approach makes it extremely uncomfortable and disturbing for those teachers who know their subjects well, who teach in ways that critically engage their students, and who want teaching to be linked to the realities of students' lives. Moreover, this "controlling, top-down" push for higher standards may actually produce a lower quality of education precisely because the tactics constrict the means by which teachers most successfully inspire students' engagement in learning and commitment to achieve (Ryan and La Guardia 1999).

The standardization of the curriculum at the state level echoes the distrust of teachers by the public and legislators—a fabricated distrust that is widely used to rally sentiment and support for high-stakes testing. Consequently, standardized testing results are used to support a principal's efforts to exercise greater power over teachers, since test scores are deemed a legitimate and objective way to measure teacher performance. The primary goal of the standardized curriculum, then, is to provide all teachers with the exact course content to which they must adhere. Hence, any variation in the quality of student performance, according to the current logic of accountability, can be tied directly to the quality of teaching. In this way, low student scores can be justified to fire teachers without further discussion, and high student scores can be used to grant merit pay to teachers as reward for their compliance.

This is an example of how a system of rewards and punishment works in schools to preserve the status quo by giving people what they need or want (i.e., salary increases) as an incentive or motivation for compliance, thereby insuring teacher regulation and social control within the classroom. However, it is imperative that we recognize that such a pervasive system of rewards and punishment is not predicated on a law of nature.

It reflects a particular ideology or set of assumptions in the education system that must be questioned, particularly when it dismantles social agency and reinforces dependence on school officials. Alfie Kohn (1993), a staunch critic of the rewards and punishment system endemic to public school practices, views this system of social control and regulation as rooted in the legacy of behaviorism and scientism:

> We are a nation that prefers acting to thinking, and practice to theory, we are suspicious of intellectuals, worshipful of technology and fixated on the bottom line. We define ourselves by numbers—take home pay, percentiles (how much does your baby weigh?), cholesterol counts, and standardized testing (how much does your child know?). By contrast we are uneasy with intangibles and unscientific abstractions such as a sense of well-being or an intrinsic motivation to learn. (9–10)

In the urgency to test students, the disempowering and negative effect of the testing situation itself and the removal of students from the classroom several times during the year for testing are seldom discussed. Such practices disrupt the developmental momentum of student learning, provoke enormous unnecessary stress and tension in students, and interfere with the quality of interaction in the classroom. In many ways, the politics of testing, along with the prescribed curriculum it inspires, ultimately erodes teacher autonomy and creativity, as well as teachers' authority within their classrooms. In the process, teachers are socialized to become highly dependent on prepackaged materials and the authority of state-sanctioned educational experts to provide the next curricular innovation.

McNeil (2000) argues that the state mechanism for assessing teacher quality, like proficiency testing, must be cheap, quick, generalizable across all subjects and school settings, and capable of being used by school-level administrators, independent of their knowledge of the subjects being taught. In many cases, what is generated is a factory-like checklist reminiscent of the social efficiency era, reducing teaching to specific, observable, and thus measurable behaviors, many having little or nothing to do with the content of the material being taught or with the particular pedagogical needs of students. Typically, behaviors found on teacher assessment checklists can include such items as eye contact with students, whether the daily objective was written on the board, whether there was a catchy opening phrase and definite closure to the lesson, and the number of times teachers varied their verbal responses to students.

A major consequence of standardized testing and teaching-to-the-test is that the emphasis of learning is transferred from intellectual activity to the dispensing of packaged fragments of information. Meanwhile, students and teachers, as subjects of classroom discourse who bring their personal stories and life experiences to bear on their teaching and learning, are systematically silenced by the need for the class to "cover" a generic curriculum at a prescribed pace established by the state. In making the case against standardized testing, Kohn (2000) argues,

> High-stakes testing has radically altered the kind of instruction that is offered in American schools, to the point that "teaching to the test" has become a prominent part of the nation's educational landscape. Teachers often feel obliged to set aside other subjects for days, weeks, or (particularly in schools serving low-income students) even months at a time in order to devote [time] to boosting students' test scores. Indeed, both the content and the format of instruction are affected; the test essentially *becomes* the curriculum. (29)

Through the hegemonic process of standardized testing, teachers, as workers, have become the new scapegoat of the system. As a result of the political struggles in education rooted in the civil rights era, it became unfashionable to blame students, their parents, or their culture. Teachers, whose status is located at the next lowest rung of the educational hierarchy (after students), became the most likely suspects. State and national teacher tests, based upon the very same premise as those administered to their students, are now being used as a primary indicator of teacher labor rather than the quality of their actual teaching. Such an assessment mechanism can now more easily be used to support the notion that the problem of student failure is the fault of poor teachers.

So, once again, educational debates have shifted from the quality of teaching and the schooling process to that of "quality control"—a shift closely linked with conservative political efforts to dictate the agenda of public education. This debate justifies taking further control of their labor away from the hands of teachers. In the process, there is no consideration for increasing classroom resources, nor are provisions made for instructional materials and ongoing teacher development linked to enhancing the quality of children's learning or teacher-parent relationships. Little attention is given to engaging communities in a plan to rectify persistent inequalities. More clearly, there is little willingness to openly challenge the asymmetrical relations of power that result in the racialized reproduction of class formations. Such a strategy must be central to efforts geared toward dismantling the educational injustices prevalent in public schools today.

The Racialized Discourse of Testing

More disturbing is the use of this system of accountability to justify the undemocratic governance of urban public schools. In many ways, the racialized discourse of the old efficiency rhetoric was refashioned into the new accountability rhetoric and quickly seized and embraced by mainstream educators and researchers who felt they were losing control of schooling debates to those who clamored for greater democratic participation by teachers, students, parents, and communities. The language of scientific accountability, with its narrow focus on test scores, was seen as a sure way to replace the messiness of "interest group" participation in schools; that is, the participation of those who had historically been excluded from the debate in the first place.

In this way, the racialized discourse of testing in public schools has historically played an insidious role in the perpetuation of underachievement among working-class and racialized student populations. Bowles and Gintis (1976) argue that

> the educational system legitimates economic inequality by providing an open, objective, and ostensibly meritocratic mechanism for assigning individuals to unequal economic positions. Through the construction of testing instruments as value-free scientific tools, considered to produce objective, measurable and quantifiable data, predefined skills and knowledge have been given priority at the expense of the cultural knowledge and experience of students from economically disenfranchised communities. (103)

As mentioned earlier, the evaluation and assessment of students (as well as teachers) is predicated on the results of standardized tests, which are used to sort, regulate, and control students. The testing of students increasingly drives the curriculum and prescribes both teaching and the role of students in their learning. This prescriptive teaching hardens and intensifies the discrimination already at work in schools, as teaching the fragmented and narrow information on the test comes to substitute for a substantive curriculum in the schools of poor and minority students. This intensified discrimination and widespread pattern of substituting test-prep materials, devoid of substantive content and respect for the ways children learn, is particularly marked in schools that serve economically oppressed communities. Hence, standardized testing has historically functioned to systematically reproduce, overtly and covertly, the conditions in schools that perpetuate a culture of elitism, privilege, and exploitation.

Among the most insidious dimensions tied to the preservation of this ideology of dominance in schools are the unexamined philosophical assumptions and values that undergird, and hence legitimate, educational policies and practices associated with standardized testing. Many of the values and assumptions at work in sustaining asymmetrical relations of power within the larger society have been engaged substantially in the work of radical educators, psychologists, sociologists, political scientists, economists, and other social critics during the last century. This chapter can do no more than provide a brief overview of some of the primary values and assumptions operating in schools. Nevertheless, it must be emphasized that the interrelatedness of these assumptions often functions in concert to successfully veil the ideological contradictions that exist between a rhetoric of democratic ideals and the racialized discourse and practices of dominance at work in U.S. public schools. Teachers may seldom connect these assumptions to their teaching practice although they underlie what teachers do in their classrooms (Kohn 1993).

An overarching philosophical assumption that undergirds the ideology of public schooling today is the unbridled, but veiled, acceptance of Darwinian conclusions related to belief in the "survival of the fittest." As a result, much educational rhetoric functions to justify the existence of economic inequality, sexism, racialized notions of humanity, and good old U.S. self-promotion at the expense of the greater good. Such rhetoric is well disguised in the false benevolence at work in the discursive justifications for standardized testing, tracking, and the competitive and instrumentalizing curricular practices found in classrooms today.

Thus, "commonsense" beliefs about human nature, deeply rooted in racialized and class notions of normalcy, are actively at work in the assessment of student intellectual abilities and their potential for academic success. For example, racialized beliefs about the inferior or superior abilities and potential of particular student populations are often utilized to justify the so-called objective measurement of student knowledge and then to use these measures to justify the unequal distribution of educational resources and opportunities. The fact that such practices effectively perpetuate class interests is well hidden by a racialized educational discourse that glorifies expediency in learning, separates theory from practice, heralds the conquest of nature, and objectifies time and human experience in the name of scientifically fabricated assessment criteria.

Also inherent in the racialized discourse of testing is an overwhelming penchant for unbridled individualism at the expense of a greater collective well-being. Hence, competition among students within the context of knowledge construction is strongly reinforced and rewarded. Students learn very quickly to acquiesce in the wiles of competition so as to be deemed worthy material for academic success in the future. In the process, knowledge is reified and objectified and students are socialized to accept that knowledge is objectively disconnected from the subjective realm of human experience. This is in contrast to a view of knowledge that connects its construction and evolution to the realities of the larger social milieu. Accordingly, students become convinced, particularly as they advance in the educational hierarchy of achievement, that their goal is to independently construct some "original" notion, thought, idea, or theory in order to gain prominence in their chosen field.

The organizational regimes of power or the hegemonic forces at work in the legitimation of knowledge and the institutional assignment of both "originality" and worthiness are seldom acknowledged. It is disturbing that the very qualities considered essential to the education of elite students and later crucial to the dicta of graduate school success are virtually absent in and almost entirely negated by standardized testing in public schools.

Further, the individualistic and economist language so prevalent in the racialized discourse of high-stakes testing is deeply rooted in the ideological tenets of advanced capitalism. Its materialist emphasis on private property is extended to the domain of knowledge, where intellectual ideas become the property of an individual or the state. Hence, the pedagogy of the elite very early teaches students that they are the owners of their intellectual products with the right to sell or buy these products at their discretion. In contrast, poor and working-class students are schooled into subordination, socialized to accept, accommodate, and comply with the knowledge deemed "truth," even when that knowledge is diametrically opposed to their experience and well-being. Academic socialization thus encourages poor students not to be creators of knowledge but to be consumers of specific knowledge forms prescribed by the dominant class. Nowhere is this prescription of knowledge for the oppressed more readily visible than in the racialized discourse of standardized testing—a prescription steeped in the rhetoric of scientism.

Scientism and Meritocracy

The scientific claim of accountability experts is one of the most devious and fallacious elements in the testing mania. An overemphasis on "hard" science and "absolute objectivity" gives rise to scientism rather than real science. Scientism refers to the power and authority vested in the mechanization of intellectual work generated by specialists. Consequently, knowledge is fragmented and instrumentalized by way of reductionist interpretations of student learning. Hence the very claim of objectivity is steeped in the cultural assumptions and racialized discourse of the dominant class.

Schools, then, operate upon a view of the world, or ideology, clearly governed by an instrumentally technocratic rationality that glorifies a logic and method based on the natural sciences. To comply with the scientific requirement of measuring knowledge, high-stakes tests are constructed under the rubric of objective knowledge. This knowledge is treated as an external body of information, produced independently of human beings and independent of time, place, and space. Thus it can be expressed in language that is technical and allegedly neutral. School knowledge becomes not only countable and measurable but also impersonal. Teaching-to-the-test thus becomes normalized and acceptable and testing is exalted as the only truly effective and "unbiased" mechanism to measure academic success and achievement.

In the process, extensive field-based research on standardized testing that has documented its negative effects on teaching and learning, particularly on disenfranchised students, is categorically ignored. Even worse is the lasting harm caused by imbedded controls, the legitimization of "accountability" as the language of school policy, and the elimination of wider public debates on the purpose of schooling for poor, working-class, and racialized students—all of which stifle concrete educational efforts to democratize schooling practices.

Scientism also supports a carte blanche adherence to the educational practice of meritocracy, which is one of the primary hegemonic mechanisms implicated in the inequitable achievement and advancement of students in the educational system. It constitutes a form of systemic control by which racialized educational discourse is naturalized and perpetuated. Public schools persistently tout the myth of scientism to guarantee that successful participation in the educational system is the most visible and legitimate process by which individuals are allocated or rewarded higher status within the society at large. Through a system of merit tied to high-stakes testing, for example, the process of unequal privilege and entitlement is successfully camouflaged under the guise of "fair and equal" opportunity for all students.

Through the daily practices of meritocracy linked to social promotion (or demotion) and graduation, a twofold justification of inequality is upheld to justify the undemocratic distribution of wealth in this country and around the world. First, it establishes the merit of those in power as the legitimate criterion for achievement and success. And second, it persists in blaming those who fail for their underachievement (whether the blame is assigned to teachers, students, or parents), by implying that they do not have the necessary intelligence, motivation, or drive to partake of what is freely being offered them by the educational system. In other words, if students fail, it's their own damn fault!

Testing and the Politics of Schooling

Within the racialized discourse of education, schools and educators, as agents of the state, are viewed as neutral and apolitical. Their sole purpose is to give students the knowledge and skills necessary to render them functional in and useful to society—in other words, to fulfill their place in the process of consumption and capitalist accumulation. Hence, ideas and practices that accord with dominant knowledge forms are generally perceived to be neutral and acceptable, shrouding the authoritarianism of the status quo. Conversely, knowledge forms that might in any way question the "official" curriculum, methods, or pedagogy are deemed "political" and unacceptable. To make things even more perplexing, opposing views are generally neutralized by a variety of social agents, including: 1. those who knowingly support the limits and configuration of "official" authority within the fundamental order of public schools for their own personal gain; 2. those who are complicit as a consequence of insufficient knowledge and skills to contest the system; 3. those who protect their class interest by "playing the game" while paying lip service to the rhetoric of helping the oppressed; and 4. those who consent due to their overwhelming fear of authority.

Unfortunately, there are many educators and advocates from all walks of life who confidently support the propagation of testing as a legitimate educational strategy in public schools, irrespective of the volumes that have been written linking standardized testing to racism and economic exploitation. The rallying cry of testing advocates is often tied to the question: "If we take away testing, how will we have the objective criteria to demand better schools?" This myopic view fails to link an acceptance and adherence to such educational policies and practices with capitalist interests that perpetuate undemocratic life in this country and around the globe. Even more disturbing is the negative impact that such practices continue to have as students are "railroaded into a testing culture that squeezes out the joy of learning and turns schools into 'factories'" (Woodward 2003). Recognizing the harmful effects of existing practices, the president of the British Association of Teachers and Lecturers argued:

> What sort of education system do we have if we brand children as failures by the time they are eleven, or worse, seven? What sort of morality is it to force on young children an impoverished curriculum diet just to help politicians meet targets and keep the Treasury happy? What difference does it really make to a child's life if he or she achieves [at certain levels] at age eleven? Will it really make them a better person, a genuinely enriched human being with a passion for learning? Of course, it won't. (Moore, cited in the *Guardian*, April 17, 2003)

In the process of attempting to rally support for their views, many well-meaning educators and advocates who are content to play the "race card" can actually obstruct teachers, parents, and communities who publicly question and critique those ideas, practices, and events that are contrary to community self-determination and the construction of a genuinely democratic political movement in education. Many go so far as to suggest that those who question racialized arguments in defense of testing as a good thing for students of color are somehow falling prey to white, bleeding-heart liberal tendencies. Radical efforts to expose the long-term damage of testing to all oppressed students are viewed as suspect. In contrast, we need to seek out a wider range of information so that we can struggle (beyond identity politics) to dismantle the structures of capitalist domination and inequality in schools and society today.

What the history of civil rights struggles in the United States should have taught us is that our understanding of racism and those schooling practices that perpetuate racialized inequality can never be separated from the reproduction of class inequality. Thus, high-stakes testing must be understood as systematically implicated in the reproduction of racialized economic inequality and injustice. For it is precisely through the uncontested acceptance of such mechanisms of social control and regulation that students from the dominant class consistently end up at the top of the hierarchy and students from subordinate communities at the bottom— which in turn readily and unjustly fuels widespread belief in the legitimacy of a hierarchically racialized, gendered, and class-stratified society.

It is no secret that in the United States the most politically powerful are those who control the bulk of society's wealth and resources. This economic and institutional control is clearly perpetuated from generation to generation through the process of schooling. The ruling class, with its bureaucratic system of managerial officials, strives to retain control of schooling through the construction of educational public policies. Thus the curriculum and pedagogical practices that support the standardization (and control) of knowledge—knowledge that functions in the interest of capitalist relations—effectively sustain the racialized educational discourse in schools. Moreover, through control of teacher certification and such schooling practices as curricular policies, literacy instruction, pedagogy, and testing requirements tied to educational opportunities, the stratification of populations so necessary to capitalist accumulation is successfully maintained. Consequently, even working-class students and students of color learn to compete furiously for the limited "top" positions in society, rather than to alter the social, political, and economic conditions that define (and limit) their future well-being and, ultimately, their destinies.

A Politics of Silence

Schools produce and perpetuate knowledge that serves as a silencing agent, in that it legitimizes the abstract reality developed by prescribed knowledge, rather than the actual lived experiences that shape the knowledge that students bring to the classroom. Nowhere was this more evident than in the response of most public schools to the events of September 11. The actual experiences of students predicated upon what they were hearing and feeling about this historical moment were marginalized and suppressed. A politics of silence was imposed in order to ensure a return to normalcy, with the expectation that there be minimal discussion about the issue. And when discussions did occur, they echoed the language of a most superficial and vulgar patriotism, in concert with the official public discourse of the government.

Consequently, blind flag-waving nationalism substituted for any real critical dialogue. Teachers were told that the attitude in classrooms was to be "business as usual" as students were being ushered in and out of their beginning-of-the-year standardized testing sessions. Meanwhile, the administrative pressure on teachers to keep up with the prescribed curriculum and to prepare students for future testing prevented critical inquiry into the initial and subsequent events connected with the "war on terrorism." So, while the practice of high-stakes testing effectively contributed to an ahistorical and fragmented response to such a significant historical event in the lives of students, booksellers were rushing to develop and insert the official historical reading into traditional social studies textbooks to generate new sales. By the time the events of September 11 and the "war on terrorism" are officially documented and taught in U.S. classrooms, the lived impact of the events will have been buried and lost for many, with only the prescribed curricula and its sanitized interpretation remaining.

Last, an aspect seldom discussed in education but very much at work in the politics of silence is the racialized discourse of "good and evil" so prevalent in conservative and liberal political discourses on schooling and society. The "good" are those who conform and seek to fulfill their rightful place in the process of capitalist accumulation. As such, the "Other" is transformed into an "evil" that must be reformed or eliminated. Albert Memmi (2000) speaks to this in his writings on racism.

> [T]he other's traits all have a negative valuation. Whatever they are, they will signify something bad. The correlative effect is that the corresponding characteristics for the one who derogates are good. We must keep this inverse relation in mind; it recurs everywhere, even where not apparent and even where the order of the terms have been changed." (95; emphasis in original)

From this perspective, all problems in schools and society are approached from the standpoint of how the "evil" (or deviance) must be eliminated in students, teachers, or parents. By linking notions of evil consequences (pregnancy, drug abuse, crime, school drop-out, unemployment, and the like) to academic failure, students who fail are justifiably excluded and rendered disposable. In the testing madness, this notion has been interjected in the definition of good schools, good students, good teachers, and good parents, where the level of "goodness" is determined by the measurable outcomes of standardized testing. The "good" are considered worthy of rewards by the state for their achievement. However, what most people fail to acknowledge is that the measures for achievement are constantly raised, in order to perpetuate the inequality inherent in the bell curve phenomenon associated with high-stakes testing.

The veiled moralism that unwittingly permeates the racialized discourse of high-stakes testing actually socializes populations to uncritically accept the inferiority of the "Other" and the need for corrective action, in order to assure the participation of the majority in the labor market and as good consumers of the nation. Hence, many unexamined assumptions shape the uncritical, commonsense perceptions of whole populations as deviant and in need of punishment or corrective action—whether this action results in the loss of academic opportunities, dead-end jobs, or incarceration. Hence, if we are to stop such manufacturing of destinies, our understanding of high-stakes testing must take on a more comprehensive historical reading of political and economic inequalities and the role of public schooling in the perpetuation of not only racism, but also class apartheid.

5

What's So Critical about Critical Race Theory?

A Conceptual Interrogation

Racism as it operates socially, in no way assumes an explicit theory of "race." (Taguieff 2001, 197)

Over the last half-century considerable attention has been paid to issues related to "race" and "race relations" in the social sciences, humanities, and legal studies. The debates intensified first with the groundbreaking *Brown v. Board of Education* case in 1954 and then again with the civil rights movements of the 1960s. The current debates are beginning to intensify once more as critical race theorists[1] not only retain the idea of "race" but further entrench it as a central category of analysis. Hence, the early "race" paradigm has become the new orthodoxy, retaining symbolic and political utility for many. This is evident in even more progressive articulations of "race" such as *The Miner's Canary*, a highly acclaimed book by Lani Guinier and Gerald Torres (2002) that enlists race as a political space within the context of what they term "a political race project."

Before continuing any further, we wish to acknowledge and commend such efforts to make sense of the problematics associated with "race" within U.S. society. However, we seek to raise different questions regarding the foundational theories that shape these arguments and, more importantly, to question the analytical limitations of "race" with respect to the formation of a critical social science and execution of progressive social policies.

97

Critical race theory emerged as an offshoot of critical legal theory. Legal scholars in this tradition argued that legal theory had historically failed to engage in a critical analysis of society and, by so doing, continued to function as a fundamental tool of oppression that ultimately benefited the state. Not long after, critical legal theory was critiqued by black critical legal scholars such as Derrick Bell, Patricia Williams, Randall Kennedy, Lani Guinier, and others who pointed to the failure of critical legal scholars to engage questions of "race" within the framework of the alternative views they posited. The result was the forging of a subdivision of critical legal theory that is now called critical race theory.

Latino critical legal scholars such as Gerald Torres and Richard Delgado, in concert with Latino scholars in education and other disciplines, followed suit by developing a field of study today known as Latino critical race theory, or LatCrit, to address similar issues within the context of Latino life in the United States. Similar critical race theory began to evolve among Asian American scholars with the work of Mari Matsuda, often considered one of the founders of the field.

Grounded in the belief that "much of the national dialogue on race relations takes place in the context of education" (Roithmayr 1999, 1), African American and Latino scholars such as Gloria Ladson-Billings, Daniel Solórzano, Dolores Delgado Bernal, and Laurence Parker began to infuse their arguments in education policy with critical race theory. Their key argument was the uncompromising insistence that "race" should occupy the central position in any legal, educational, or social policy analysis. Given the centrality assigned to "race," "racial" liberation was embraced as not only the primary but as the most significant objective of any emancipatory vision of education or the larger society.

The Centrality of "Race"

There is no question but that the issues raised by critical race theorists in education, policy studies and the social sciences are significant to our understanding of the conditions that plague racialized student populations in U.S. schools today. However, one of our major concerns with the use of critical race theory to buttress educational-political debates of racialized oppression or racism is directly linked to the use of "race" as the central unit of analysis. Coupled with an uncompromising emphasis on "race" is the conspicuous absence of a systematic discussion of class and, more importantly, a substantive critique of capitalism.

Let us be more specific here. In contending with questions of "race" and institutional power, references are indeed made to "capitalism" or "class"[2] in some works by critical race theorists and, in particular, Latino critical race theorists, who acknowledge that "attention to class issues has been . . . a pending, but as yet underdeveloped, trajectory in the future evolution of LatCrit theory and the consolidation of LatCrit social justice agendas" (Iglesias 1999, 64).[3] However, these efforts to explore the ways in which socioeconomic interests are expressed in the law or education are generally vague and undertheorized. Because of this lack of a theoretically informed account of racism and capitalist social relations, critical race theory has done little to further our understanding of the political economy of racism and racialization. In addition, much of critical race theory's approach is informed by ambiguous ideas of "institutional racism" or "structural racism," which, as Miles (1989) points out, are problematic due to the danger of conceptual inflation.

Our aim here is not to dismiss this important body of work but to point out an important analytical distinction we make in our intellectual and political project. Our analysis of racism in contemporary society begins with the capitalist mode of production, classes, and class struggle. The mode of production, which is the site of class relations, is the point of departure in our interrogation of racism as an ideology of social exclusion. In contrast, critical race scholars attribute constitutive power to the American legal system itself. Hence, the "relative autonomy" of legal institutions is invoked to stress the power of "race" and to set their work apart from critical legal scholars, who "could not come to grips with the continuing problems of deeply embedded racism" (Guinier and Torres 2002, 34). We maintain that the legal system (the state) is located in a given economic context and is shaped by the imperatives of capital.[4]

Our critique, then, is tied to the continued use of the traditional language of social theory, which has always been inadequate in problematizing notions of "race" in both research and popular discourse. In essence, we argue that the use of "race" has been elevated to a theoretical construct, despite the fact that the concept of "race" itself has remained under-theorized. Hence, to employ alternative constructs derived from legal theory to shape arguments related to educational policy and institutional practices, although well meaning and eloquent, is like beating a dead horse. No matter how much is said, it is impossible to enliven or extend the debate on educational policy with its inherent inequalities by using the language of "race."

Even a brief overview of the most prominent writings in critical race theory shows how little movement there has been in furthering our understanding of the concept or redirecting the debate. Overall, most of the work is anchored in the popular intersectionality argument of the poststructuralist and postmodernist era, which maintains that "race," gender, and class should all receive equal attention in our understanding of society and our development of institutional policies and practices. More recently, Guinier and Torres (2002), in an apparent effort to push through the limits of the intersectionality argument, proposed to advocate for what they term "racial literacy" from which "to identify patterns of injustice that link race to class, gender, and other forms of power." (29) Despite their innovative use of "race," its traditional analytical use remains intact.

Our concerns with critical race theory go beyond the desire to construct intellectual abstractions. Rather, our concerns are grounded in political questions such as: Where exactly does an antirace theory of society lead us in real political struggles for social justice, human rights, and economic democracy? How do we launch a truly universal emancipatory political project anchored primarily upon a theory of "race"? Where is a critique of capitalism or an explicit anticapitalist vision in a critical theory of "race"? Can we afford to overlook the inherent existence of a politics of identity in the foundational views that led to the construction of critical race theory? We are also troubled by the confusion with respect to the terms critical race theorists use to frame their analysis.

In this context, it is important to distinguish between how we understand the construct of "race" and its genesis. In our analysis, "race," simply put, is the child of racism. That is to say, racism does not exist because there is such a thing as "race." Rather, notions of "race" are a fundamental ideological construction of racism or a racialized interpretation of phenotypically and, may we add, regionally different human beings. The process of racialization, then, is at work in all relations in a capitalist society. Alternatively, we might say that the empire is not built on "race" but on an ideology of racism—this being one of the primary categories by which human beings are sorted, controlled, and made disposable at the point of production.

Hence, the experience of alienation is shaped along a variety of variables, one of which is that of racialization or racialized class relations. Racism is one of the primary ideologies by which material conditions in society are organized and perpetuated in the service of capitalist accumulation. This is why, to repeat, the empire is not built on "race" but on a variety of ideologies (of which racism is one) that justify the exploitation and domination of populations deemed as "Other" so as to conserve the capitalist social order.

We also seek to interrogate the idea of "race" as culture. For example, instead of linking the notion of culture to class relations which emerge at the point of production, or to the relations of production in which human beings exist and survive, critical race theorists link culture to the idea of "race"—an idea that historically has been associated with phenotypical traits. In the new "race" orthodoxy, phenotypical traits remain central to social construction, shared histories, and social narratives defined by experiences that are phenotypically determined. Miles (1989) associates this discourse of "race" to the process of signification:

> [W]hen the idea of "race" is employed, it is the result of signification whereby certain somatic characteristics are attributed with meaning and are used to organise populations into groups which are defined as "races." People differentiated on the basis of the signification of phenotypical features are usually also represented as possessing certain cultural characteristics, with the result that the population is represented as exhibiting a specific profile of biological and cultural attributes. The deterministic manner of this representation means that all those who possess the signified phenotypical characteristics are assumed to possess the additional characteristics. (71)

Narrative and Storytelling as Method

The process of signification is at work in the emphasis that critical race theory places on "experiential knowledge" (Delgado 1995; Ladson-Billings 1999). Robin Barnes (1990) notes that "Critical race theorists . . . integrate their experiential knowledge, drawn from a shared history as 'Other' with their ongoing struggles to transform a world deteriorating under the albatross of racial hegemony" (1864–65). In concert with this privileging of experience, critical race theory employs narratives and storytelling as a central method of inquiry to "analyze the myths, presuppositions, and received wisdoms that make up the common culture about race and that invariably render blacks and other minorities one-down" (Delgado 1995, xiv). The results of this storytelling method are theorized and then utilized to draw conclusions meant to impact public policy and institutional practices.

The narrative and storytelling method employed by critical race theorists sought to critique essentialist narratives in law, education, and the social sciences. In place of a systematic analysis of class and capitalist relations, critical race theory constructs "race"-centered responses to Eurocentrism and white privilege. Delgado Bernal (2002) affirms the validity of this position, arguing that

> Western modernism is a network or grid of broad assumptions and beliefs that are deeply embedded in the way dominant Western culture constructs the nature of the world and one's experiences in it. In the United States, the center of this grid is a Eurocentric epistemological perspective based on White privilege. (111)

The narrative method based on this perspective "has become especially successful among groups committed to making the voice of the voiceless heard in the public arena" (Viotti da Costa 2001, 21). However, despite an eagerness to include the participation of historically excluded populations, scholars who embrace the poetics of the narrative approach often "fail to challenge the underlying socioeconomic, political and cultural structures that have excluded these groups to begin with and have sustained the illusion of choice" (Watts 1991, 652). Thus, the narrative and storytelling approach can render the scholarship antidialectical by creating a false dichotomy between objectivity and subjectivity, "forgetting that one is implied in the other, [while ignoring] a basic dialectical principle: that men and women make history, but not under the conditions of their own choosing" (Viotti da Costa 2001, 20).

We agree that "cultural resources and funds of knowledge such as myths, folk tales, *dichos*, *consejos*, kitchen talk, [and] autobiographical stories" (Delgado Bernal 2002, 120) employed by critical race theory can illuminate particular concrete manifestations of racism. However, we contend that they can also prove problematic in positing a broader understanding of the fundamental macrosocial dynamics which shape the conditions that give rise to the "micro-aggressions" (Solórzano 1998) of racism in the first place. In an incisive critique of the narrative approach, Emilia Viotti da Costa (2001) argues,

> The new paths it opened for an investigation of the process of construction and articulation of multiple and often contradictory identities (ethnic, class, gender, nationality and so on), often led to the total neglect of the concept of class as an interpretive category. . . . What started as . . . a critique of Marxism, has frequently led to a complete subjectivism, to the denial of the possibility of knowledge and sometimes even to the questioning of the boundaries between history and fiction, fact and fancy." (19)

Robin Kelley, in his book *Yo' Mama's DisFUNKtional* (1997), offers the following illuminating and sobering commentary regarding the limits of personal experience and storytelling:

> I am not claiming absolute authority or authenticity for having lived there. On the contrary, it is because I did not know what happened to our world, to my neighbors, my elders, my peers, our streets, buildings, parks, our health, that I chose not to write a memoir. Indeed, if I relied on memory alone I would invariably have more to say about devouring Good and Plentys or melting crayons on the radiator than about economic restructuring, the disappearance of jobs, and the dismantling of the welfare state. (4–5)

Hence, we believe the use of critical race theory in education and the social sciences in general, despite authors' intentions, can unwittingly serve purposes that are fundamentally conservative or mainstream at best. Three additional but related concerns with the storytelling narrative method are also at issue here. One is the tendency to romanticize the experience of marginalized groups, privileging the narratives and discourses of "people of color," solely based on their experience of oppression, as if a people's entire politics can be determined solely by their individual location in history. The second is the tendency to dichotomize and "overhomogenize" both "white" people and "people of color" with respect to questions of voice and political representation (Viotti da Costa 2001). And the third, anticipated by C. L. R. James in 1943,[5] is the inevitable "exaggerations, excesses and ideological trends for which the only possible name is chauvinism" (McLemee 1996, 86). Unfortunately, these tendencies, whether academic or political, can result in unintended essentialism and superficiality in our theorizing of broader social inequalities, as well as the solutions derived from such theories.

Yet, truth be told, prescribed views of humanity are seldom the reality, whatever be their source. Human beings who share phenotypical traits seldom respond to the world within the constraints of essentialized expectations and perceptions. Hence, any notion of "racial" solidarity "must run up against the hard facts of political economy . . . and enormous class disparities" within racialized communities (Gates 1997, 36). This is why Gilroy (2000) warns against "short-cut solidarity" attitudes that assume that a person's political allegiance can be determined by his or her "race" or that a "shared history" will guarantee an emancipatory worldview. For this reason, we argue that such declarations, though they may sound reasonable, commonsensical, or even promising as literary contributions, have little utility in explaining "how and why power is constituted, reproduced and transformed" (Viotti da Costa 2001, 22).

Identity Politics and the Mantra of Intersectionality

Since the 1970s, much of the progressive literature on subordinate cultural populations has utilized the construct of "race" as a central category of analysis for interpreting social conditions of inequality and marginalization. In turn, this literature has adhered to a perspective of "race" as identity. This "raced" identity has received overwhelming attention in both the sociological and political arenas. Unfortunately, the unrelenting emphasis on "identity" unleashed a barrage of liberal and conservative political movements that unwittingly undermined the socialist project of emancipation in this country and abroad. Radical mass organizations that had once worked to spearhead actions for economic democracy, human rights, and social justice were crippled by the fury. In the midst of the blinding celebratory affirmations of identity, neoliberal efforts to seize greater dominion over international markets proliferated and globalization became the policy buzzword of U.S. economic imperialism at the end of the twentieth century.

Given this legacy, it is not surprising that many of the theories, practices, and policies that inform the social science analysis of racialized populations today are overwhelmingly rooted in a politics of identity. Consequently, this approach—steeped in deeply insular perspectives of "race" and representation—has often ignored the imperatives of capitalist accumulation and the presence of class divisions among racialized populations, even though, as John Michael (2000) reminds us, "identity categories and groups are always [racialized] and gendered and inflected by class" (29).

As we have previously stated, much of the literature on critical race theory lacks a substantive analysis of class and a critique of capitalism. And when class issues are mentioned, the emphasis is usually on an undifferentiated plurality that intersects with multiple oppressions. Unfortunately, this "new pluralism" fails to grapple with the relentless totalizing dimension of capitalism and its overwhelming tendency to homogenize rather than to diversify human experience (Wood 1994).

Strongly influenced by a politics of identity, critical race theorists incorporate the intersectionality argument[6] to refer to their examination of race, sex, class, national origin, and sexual orientation and how the combination of these identities plays out in various settings (Delgado and Stefancic 2001). This school of thought, common to progressive scholarship, generally includes a laundry list of oppressions (race, class, gender, homophobia, and the like) that are to be engaged with equal weight in the course of ascribing pluralized sensibilities to any political project that proposes to theorize social inequalities. Hence, inadvertently in the name of recognizing and celebrating difference and diversity, this analytical construct reduces "the capitalist system (or the 'economy') to one of many spheres in the plural and heterogeneous complexity of modern society" (Wood 1995, 242).

Wood argues that the intersectionality argument represents a distorted appropriation of Antonio Gramsci's notion of "civil society," which was explicitly intended to function as a weapon against capitalism by identifying potential spaces of freedom outside the state for autonomous, voluntary organization and plurality. However, as used by many on the left to link multiple oppressions to specific plural identities, the concept has been stripped of its unequivocal, anticapitalist intent. Wood speaks to the danger inherent in this analytical twist.

> Here, the danger lies in the fact that the totalizing logic and the coercive power of capitalism is reduced to one set of institutions and relations among many others, on a conceptual par with households or voluntary associations. Such a reduction is, in fact, the principal distinctive feature

of "civil society" in its new incarnation. Its effect is to conceptualize away the problem of capitalism, by disaggregating society into fragments, with no overarching power structure, no totalizing unity, no systemic coercion—in other words, no capitalist system, with its expansionary drive and its capacity to penetrate every aspect of social life. (Wood 1995, 245)

This denial of the totalizing force of capitalism does not simply substantiate the existence of plural identities and relations that should be equally privileged and given weight as modes of domination. The logic of this argument fails to recognize that "the class relation that constitutes capitalism is not, after all, just a personal identity, nor even just a principle of 'stratification' or inequality. It is not only a specific system of power relations but also the constitutive relation of a distinctive social process, the dynamic of accumulation and the self-expansion of capital" (Wood 1995, 246).

Furthermore, such logic ignores the fact that notions of identity result from a process of identification with a particular configuration of historically lived or transferred social arrangements and practices tied to material conditions of actual or imagined survival. The intersectionality argument fails to illuminate the manner in which commonly identified diverse social spheres or plural identities exist "within the determinative force of capitalism, its system of social property relations, its expansionary imperatives, its drive for accumulation, its commodification of all social life, its creation of the market as a necessity, and so on" (Wood 1995, 246).

There is no question but that racism as an ideology is integral to the process of capital accumulation. The failure to confront this dimension in an analysis of contemporary society as a racialized phenomenon or to continue to treat class as merely one of a multiplicity of (equally valid) perspectives, which may or may not "intersect" with the process of racialization, is a serious shortcoming. In addressing this issue, we must recognize that even progressive African American and Latino scholars and activists have often used identity politics, which generally glosses over class differences and/or ignores class contradictions, in an effort to build a political base. Constructions of "race" are objectified and mediated as truth to ignite political support, divorced from the realities of class struggle. By so doing, race-centered scholars have unwittingly perpetuated the vacuous and dangerous notion that politics and economics are two separate spheres of society which function independently—a view that firmly anchors and sustains prevailing class relations of power in society.

Separation of the Political and Economic

One of our greatest concerns with the way notions of "race" and "race relations" have evolved over time, including the most recent arguments for a critical race theory, is the fact that political and economic spheres continue to remain separate in traditional analytical treatments of "race." In shedding light on the impact of such a practice, we turn once again to the work of Wood (1995) who argues that "there has been a tendency to perpetuate the rigid conceptual separation of the 'economic' and 'political' which has served capitalist ideology so well ever since the classical economist discovered the 'economy' in the abstract and began emptying capitalism of its social and political content" (19).

In essence, Wood attempts to reveal the way this false separation of the political and economic has served to obscure and distort our understanding of the fragmentation of social life within capitalism. Michael Parenti's (1995) work similarly exposes the class-driven interests of the economy, hidden under its abstraction.

> The economy itself is not a neutral entity. Strictly speaking, there is no such thing as "the economy." Nobody has ever seen or touched the economy. What we see are people engaged in the exchange of values, in productive and not such productive labor, and we give an overarching name to all these activities, calling them "the economy," a hypothetical construct imposed on observable actualities. We then often treat our abstractions as reified entities, as self-generating forces of their own. So we talk about the problems of the economy in general terms, not the problems of the capitalist economy with a specific set of social relations and a discernable distribution of class power. The economy becomes an embodied entity unto itself. (81)

Traditional and popular conceptual formations utilized down to the present day to define "race" within the United States have likewise concealed the deeply embedded relationship between racism and class. For this reason, Miles and Brown (2003) assert that one of the major analytical tasks before us is "the historical (as opposed to abstract theoretical) investigation of the interpolation of racialisation and racism in political and economic relations" (137).

The separation of economic and political spheres was underscored in the civil rights movements of the 1960s and 1970s. Although these movements sought to address the impoverished material conditions of African Americans and other economically oppressed populations, their emphasis on a liberal, rights-centered political agenda undermined the development of a coherent working-class movement in the United States. Unfortunately, the opposition to a class-based politics, resulting from an ideological separation of economic and political spheres, solidified the division between economic and political action—a division inherent in capitalist appropriation and exploitation. As Wood (1995) suggests, "This 'structural' separation may, indeed, be the most effective defense mechanism available to capital" (20).

Our opposition to the separation of political and economic spheres is in concert with Marx's notion that the ultimate secret of capitalist production is a political one. The key to Marx's argument is that the well-camouflaged continuity between what we term economic and political spheres be exposed. In Marxist analysis, the economy is viewed as a set of social relations. This view is in sharp contrast with classical views of the economy that "fail to treat the productive sphere itself as defined by social determinations and in effect deal with society 'in the abstract'" (Wood 1995, 22). Consequently, when theories of "race," racism, and other forms of inequality are informed by liberal perspectives of the economy, their critical edge is eroded and they are easily assimilated into mainstream ideologies that retreat from class concerns.

Contrary to such perspectives, we argue for a materialist understanding of the world in which we grapple forthrightly with the impact of racism upon our lives. This entails understanding two significant principles of analysis. The first requires us to engage the social relations and practices by which human beings interact with nature and which are thereby implicated in producing the life conditions we are seeking to remedy. And second, we seek a historical understanding of human life that recognizes all products of social activity and all social interactions between human beings as material forces. All social forms, including those that sustain racism, as well as other forms of social inequalities, are products of a particular social system of production. Wood (1995) sheds light on this relationship by linking the mode of production to questions of power relations and exploitation.

> A mode of production is not simply a technology but a social organi-
> zation of productive activity, and a mode of exploitation is a relation-
> ship of power. Furthermore, the power relationship that conditions the
> nature and extent of exploitation is a matter of political organization
> within and between contending classes. In the final analysis the rela-
> tion between appropriators and producers rests on the relative strength
> of classes, and this is largely determined by the internal organization
> and the political forces with which each enters into the class struggle.
> (27)

Hence, all forms of social inequality are defined by class relations or motivated by the persistent drive to perpetuate class inequality within the
context of the capitalist state, a phenomenon perpetuated by the ongoing
construction and reconstruction of capitalist class relations. Thus, racism
is operationalized through racialized class relations. Sexism is operationalized through gendered class relations. Heterosexism is operationalized through homophobic class relations. All these function in concert to
sustain cultural, political, and economic stratification within societies at
large.

To reiterate, everything functions within the context of material conditions—whether one is talking about psychological, corporeal, or spiri-
tual dimensions of culture. We understand culture as a social phenomenon produced at the point of production through the particular configuration of social-material relations found within the nation-state, which
include the particularities of the region's historical, social-material
arrangements and organization.

Given this perspective, class is implicated in all social arrangements
of oppression, including racism. Nothing occurs without implicating
the material conditions that shape the way individuals and groups locate themselves (and are located) in the context of the body politic
of the nation-state. What, then, is the motivating force for the construction of particular social arrangements, whether these are marked
by physical, national, or ideological signifiers? Simply put, it is the
exploitation and domination of the majority of the population in the
interest of sustaining the power of capital. This is inextricably tied to

retaining dominion over the world's populations and natural resources by the ruling elite.

Capitalist class relations, both anchored in and camouflaged by the precepts of modernity, are constructed in the historical, social-material milieu of each nation-state at the moment of colonization, by way of the introduction of capitalist modes of production into each region. Consequently, questions of the economy and politics are inextricably linked and cannot be separated. Hence, to speak of the political sphere as being separate from the economic is to create a false abstract notion that fundamentally serves the interests of capitalist relations and the accumulative drive for capital and power by the few. This abstract separation conceals the unjust accumulation of capital and power—an accumulation sustained by asymmetrical relations tied to class and firmly anchored to the social practices of racism, sexism, homophobia, ethnocentrism, and other forms of social inequality.

White Supremacy and the Intractability of Racism

James Baldwin argues, in his 1984 essay "On Being 'White' . . . and Other Lies," "No one was white before he/she came to America. It took generations, a vast amount of coercion, before this became a white country" (Baldwin 1998, 178). Baldwin's words clearly point to the artificial construction of a "black-white" paradigm for organizing power in America. We argue that this racialized construction of power was (and continues to be) predicated upon the political economic imperatives of capitalism, rather than an essentialized and intractable white supremacy.

Although a goal of critical race theory is to eliminate "racial oppression" as part of a larger effort to end all forms of oppression (Tate 1997), a central tenet of this perspective is that "race" is an essential reality of life and racism a permanent feature of social relations in the modern world. Hence, critical race theorists and their supporters uncompromisingly adhere not only to a belief in the existence of "races" but also to the "normalcy" of racism. For example, Ladson-Billings (1999) explains that critical race theory begins with the view that

> racism is "normal, not aberrant, in American society" (Delgado 1995, xiv). . . . Indeed, Bell's major premise in *Faces at the Bottom of the Well* (1992) is that racism is a permanent fixture of American life. Thus, the

strategy becomes one of unmasking and exposing racism in its various permutations. (12)

This belief in the permanence of racism is coupled with the notion of white supremacy in the literature on critical race theory. Major writings in the field (Wing 1997; Crenshaw et al. 1995; Delgado 1995; Bell 1992) highlight two central unifying ideas. The first is to understand how a "regime of white supremacy and its subordination of people of color have been created and maintained in America" (Crenshaw et al. 1995, xiii); and the second is "to change the bond that exists between law [or institutions] and racial power" (Ladson-Billings 1999, 14). It is important to note that, although mention is made of changing the law and other societal institutions such as schools, the change is first and foremost concerned with the idea of "racial power," preserving the centrality of "race."

Hence, in their efforts to sort out the complexities of "race" problems in America, critical race theorists and many prominent intellectuals place an emphasis on the notion of white supremacy. For example, Villenas, Deyhle, and Parker (1999) speak of education as "the greatest normalizer of White supremacy" (48). The writings of bell hooks illustrate the common use in critical race theory of the term "white supremacy" when addressing the racialized inequalities suffered by African Americans. In *Talking Back* (1989), hooks explains the shift in her language.

> I try to remember when the word racism ceased to be the term which best expressed for me the exploitation of black people and people of color in this society and when I began to understand that the most useful term was white supremacy . . . the ideology that most determines how white people in this society perceive and relate to black people and other people of color. (112–13)

hooks's explanation illustrates both her belief in the existence of a "white" ideology that has "black" people as its primary object (despite her mention of "people of color") and the reification of skin color as the most active determinant of social relations between "black" and "white" populations. The persistence of such notions of racialized exploitation and domination privileges one particular form of racism while ignoring the historical and contemporary oppression of populations who have been treated as distinct and inferior "races" without the necessary reference to skin color.

Moreover, white supremacy arguments essentialize "black-white" relations by inferring that the inevitability of skin color ensures the reproduction of racism in the "postcolonial" world, where "white people" predominantly associate "black people" with inferiority. Delgado Bernal (2002) expresses this view in her discussion of a "Eurocentric perspective" when she writes: "Traditionally, the majority of Euro-Americans adhere to a Eurocentric perspective founded on covert and overt assumptions [of] White supremacy" (111).

This view fails to recognize the precolonial origins of racism, which were structured in Europe by the development of nation-states and capitalist relations of production. "The dichotomous categories of Black as victims, and Whites as perpetrators of racism, tend to homogenize the objects of racism, without paying attention to the different experience of men and women, of different social classes and ethnicities" (Anthias and Yuval-Davis 1992, 15). As such, there is little room to link, with equal legitimacy and analytical specificity the continuing struggles against racism by Jews, Romas, the Irish, immigrant workers, refugees, and other racialized populations of the world (including Africans racialized by Africans) to the struggle of African Americans.

Theories of racism based on racialized ideas of "white supremacy" ultimately adhere to a "race relations" paradigm. Thus, these theories anchor racialized inequality to the alleged "nature" of "white people" and the psychological influence of "white ideology" on both "whites" and "blacks," rather than to the complex nature of historically constituted social relations of power and their material consequences. In light of this, hooks's preference for "white supremacy" (although, more recently, she links it to both patriarchal and capitalist formations) represents a perspective that, despite its oppositional intent and popularity among activists and critical race scholars, fails to advance an understanding of the debilitating structures of capitalism and the nature of class formations within a racialized, gendered world. More specifically, the struggle against racism and class inequality cannot be founded on either academic or popularized notions of "race" or "white supremacy"—notions that ultimately reify and "project a 'phantom objectivity,' an autonomy that seems so strictly rational and all-embracing as to conceal every trace of its fundamental nature" (Radin, cited in Harris 1998, 107). Rather than working to invert racist notions of racialized inferiority, antiracist scholars and activists should seek to develop a class-based critical theory of racism.

Our contention with the critical race theorists is that they remain silent about capitalist production relations in the midst of their often-repeated intersectionality mantra of class, race, and gender. However, it is not our intention to resurrect the race-versus-class debate of the last several decades. Instead, we seek to place the political, economic, and ideological process of capitalist social relations at the center of an understanding of racialized inequalities. Moreover, we find no theoretical or empirical reasons for legitimizing the ideological notion of "race" or "white supremacy" by promoting these ideas as central analytical categories. On the contrary, as Balibar (2003) suggests, an "after race" position must be something more substantial. It must challenge "the idea that there is *no end to racism in history*" (18).

Reframing the Politics of Racism

In order to begin reframing the politics of racism, it is necessary to construct a new language with which to articulate the conditions of exclusion, exploitation, and domination in the world. As activists and social scientists, we must begin this effort in our scholarship and our political practice by deconstructing "common sense categories and [setting] up rigorous analytic concepts in their place. Here, it appears to us that an excessively vague use of the vocabulary of race should be rejected, and that one should resist the extensions which banalise the evil, or remove its specificity" (Wieviorka 1997, 40). More specifically, we must begin by shattering our "race fixation."

However, despite the dangerous distortions that arise from the use of "race" as a central analytical category, most scholars seem unable to break with the hegemonic tradition of its use in the social sciences. Our efforts to problematize the reified nature of the term "race" and eliminate it as a metaphor in our work are met with resistance, even by progressive intellectuals of all communities. This resistance is expressed through anxiety, trepidation, and anger. Even merely questioning the existence of "races" is often met with greater suspicion than liberal notions that perpetuate a deficit view of "race."

Oliver Cox, in his 1948 treatise on "race relations," for example, posits that "it would probably be as revealing of [negative] interracial attitudes to deliberate upon the variations in the skeletal remains of some people as it would be to question an on-going society's definition of a race because, anthropometrically speaking, the assumed race is not a *real* race" (Cox 1970, 319).[7] Similarly, in a more recent work, *The Racial Contract*, Charles Mills (1997) argues that "the only people who can find it psychologically possible to deny the centrality of race are those who are racially privileged, for whom race is invisible precisely because the world is structured around them, whiteness as the grounds against which the figures of other races—those who, unlike us, are raced—appear" (76).

Inherent in these commentaries is the refusal to consider that the denial of "races" does not imply the denial of racism or the racist ideologies that have been central to capitalist exploitation and domination around the globe. The failure to grasp this significant analytical distinction ultimately stifles the development of a critical theory of racism, one with the analytical depth to free us from a paradigm that explains social subordination (or domination) by the alleged "nature" of particular populations.

Visceral and uncritical responses to eliminating the concept of "race" are often associated with a fear of delegitimizing the historical movements for liberation that have been principally defined in terms of "race" struggles, or progressive institutional interventions that have focused on "race" numbers to evaluate success. Although understandable, such responses demonstrate the tenacious and adhesive quality of socially constructed ideas and show how these ideas, through their historical usage, become commonsense notions that resist deconstruction. The dilemma for scholars and activists in the field is well articulated by Angela Davis (1996).

> "Race" has always been difficult to talk about in terms not tainted by ideologies of racism, with which the notion of "race" shares a common historical evolution. The assumption that a taxonomy of human populations can be constructed based on phenotypical characteristics has been discredited. Yet, we continue to use the term "race," even though many of us are very careful to set it off in quotation marks to indicate that while we do not take seriously the notion of "race" as biologically grounded, neither are we able to think about racist power structures and marginalization processes without invoking the socially constructed concept of "race." (43)

Consequently, "race" has been retained as "an analytical category, not because it corresponds to any biological or epistemological absolutes, but because of the power that collective identities acquire" (Gilroy 1991, 9). This power requires that racialized identities be accepted as commonplace and as central to political struggle, despite the constructed limitations that belie their utility.

Terry Eagleton (2000) asserts, "There can be no political emancipation for our time which is not at some level indebted to the Enlightenment" (65). In agreement, we posit that reframing a politics of racism requires us to rethink one of the fundamental critiques of the Enlightenment made by many progressive theorists, including those at the forefront of critical race theory. The demise of the metanarrative in the late twentieth century cleared the way for the "new pluralism." Tied to this politics of diversity was the eradication of any assumptions that supported the existence of universal principles of rights sufficiently undifferentiated to accommodate diverse identities and lifestyles. The increasing fragmentation of social relations and personal identities were thought to require more complex pluralistic principles that recognized the plurality of oppressions or forms of domination. The socialist emancipatory project was rejected in favor of what was considered to be the more inclusive category of democracy, a concept that essentially treats all oppressions equally. These theories were posited as being more in tune with the complexity of human diversity than those that "privileged" class relations or "reduced" all oppressions to class struggle.

However politically progressive such a view might seem, its results were disastrous to the development of a truly expansive emancipatory movement and the forging of an economically democratic society. As Eagleton (2000) reminds us,

> A classless society can be achieved only by taking class identifications seriously, not by a liberal pretense that they do not exist. The most uninspiring kind of identity politics are those which claim that an already fully fledged identity is being repressed by others. The more inspiring forms are those in which you lay claim to an equality with others in being free to determine what you might wish to become. Any authentic affirmation of difference thus has a universal dimension. (66)

In the absence of this "universal dimension," social movements principally grounded in identity politics—despite appalling material inequalities—resulted in an uncritical acceptance of capitalist expansion.

Consequently, the final years of the twentieth century were marked by one of the greatest moments of capitalist expansion, shrouded in the rhetoric of globalization—an economic expansionism carried out with few political restraints or legal reprisal by the myriad of identity movements all busy vying for their piece of the pie. While the new pluralism aspired to create a democratic community that could embrace and celebrate all social formations of difference—with its mantra of "race, gender, and class"—it failed to acknowledge the possibility that these differences could also encompass relations of exploitation and domination. Thus, advocates of the "new pluralism" failed to recognize several deadly fundamental realities of class relations: 1. it can exist only within structures of inequality; 2. all social oppressions are fundamentally linked to class within the context of capitalist relations of power; and 3. differences within groups also "proliferate along the obvious axes of division: gender, age, sexuality, region, class, wealth and health . . . [challenging] the unanimity of racialized collectivities" (Gilroy 2000, 24).

The "new pluralism" opened the door to the carte blanche dismissal of class analysis and the unbridled impact of capitalism on people's lives. In its place, hidden narratives of distinct collectivities evolved along with essentialized notions that often shaped new forms of social tyranny for those perceived as "Other" within the context of antiracism. In the name of conserving the right to difference and oppositionality, such narratives also eroded the sustained solidarity of diverse sectors of the population both from within and without. Underpinning these movements was the goal of stripping away the Enlightenment metanarrative of universal humanity. Without this metanarrative, as Jeffrey Isaac (1992) argues, theory lost its sense of purpose: "If there are no metanarratives, no underlying reasons for us to do what we should do then the theorist or political writer is under no obligation to offer such reasons in support of his or her proposal. Theory then becomes rhetoric, or poetry, or perhaps a game in which the writer's will to power or self-expression becomes his or her primary motivation" (8–9).

Instead, we firmly believe that to reframe the politics of racism in society today requires a willingness to resurrect the Enlightenment tradition within a historical process as posited by Marx. "By putting a critique of political economy in place of uncritical submission to the assumptions and categories of capitalism, he made it possible to see within it the conditions of its suppression by a more humane society" (Wood 1995, 177).

These categories of political economy devised and articulated by Marx are requisite conceptual tools in understanding racism in contemporary capitalist societies. One of the major objectives of this volume and in particular this chapter has been to show that the retention of "race" as a discursive or analytic category is seriously problematic. Moreover, an attempt to develop a "critical theory of race" or a LatCrit methodology will in effect reproduce a specious concept which has no theoretical or analytical value. Also, the widely employed notion of *intersectionality* is equally problematic where a multitude of oppressions and identities are assigned "equivalent" explanatory power outside class relations. As we posit in our introduction, to treat the category of class as just another "ism" as many LatCrit writers do is simplistic and misguided. The concept of class is located within production relations and represents a very different and unique structural feature in a capitalist political economy.

As we have attempted here, the terrain occupied by critical race and LatCrit scholars must and can be contested. The task for all anti-racist scholars is to focus on *racism as an ideology* and *racism as a relation of production*. Such an interrogation requires a renewed historical materialist method informed by Marx's writings, most notably the preface to *A Contribution to the Critique of Political Economy*. Thus, this analysis leads us to locate the capitalist mode of production at the center of a theory of racism and class inequality. Finally, the theoretical argument that we offer is that any account of contemporary racism(s) and related exclusionary practices divorced from an explicit engagement with racialization and its articulation with the reproduction of capitalist relations of production is incomplete. The continued neglect by critical race theorists to treat with theoretical *specificity* the political economy of racialized class inequalities is a major limitation in an otherwise significant and important body of literature.

6

Mapping Latino Studies

Critical Reflections
on Class and Social Theory

In serious, critical work, there are no "absolute beginnings" and
few unbroken continuities. (Hall 1980, 2)

The conservative climate befalling universities across the
United States raises serious concerns for the future of Latino studies. This
is particularly true where university discourse, victim to its own political
retrenchment, wrongly concludes that questions of culture, race, diversity, and multiculturalism were sufficiently attended to in the post–civil
rights era. Correspondingly, as the multicultural or diversity rhetoric of
the university wanes in the marketplace of ideas, raising dollars emerges
as the top priority for universities nationwide—a feat accomplished primarily by adjusting faculty scholarship and research agendas to coincide
with the priorities and mandates of the corporate world. In the main,
many academic departments and university policy centers or "think
tanks," almost entirely dependent on corporate monies, advance research
priorities and policy "solutions" that, in the final analysis, serve the needs
of capital. The impact of such measures is, unfortunately, to render progressive Latino studies scholars virtually invisible, in efforts to shape the
policy debate.[1]

The social project of Latino studies has been deemed intellectually suspect, as original analysis and innovative research and teaching approaches are sharply eclipsed by a revamped emphasis on traditional pedagogy and positivist scientific methods. Here we are referring to reduc-
tionistic, instrumentalized, and fragmented methods of inquiry and
teaching that, historically, have been most responsible for promoting in-

tellectual parochialism (i.e., teacher-centered lecture format or the dominance of psychological paradigms in education). Consequently, critical comparative studies and collaborative interdisciplinary efforts to construct a full-bodied knowledge of Latino life and thought are often discouraged by those who continue to privilege the narrow rationality of quantitative enthusiasts.

Latino studies scholarship within the humanities, for example, can seldom forge a solid relationship with the social sciences, nor can either field readily establish a foothold in the "hard" sciences of physics, mathematics, or the "applied" disciplines. Hence, despite recent seismic paradigm shifts that have challenged positivist claims regarding a single, fixed truth or scientific grand narratives to justify cause and effect interpretations, there is still a compelling need to break down the strictures of discipline-specific knowledge construction. To accomplish this, we argue that Latino studies needs to move more vigorously toward what Bob Jessop and Ngai-Ling Sum (2001) and Andrew Sayer (1999) term a post-disciplinary approach to our teaching and research in the field—an approach that extends inquiry beyond disciplinary boundaries by following a coherent group of "ideas and connections wherever they lead instead of following them only as far as the border of [the] discipline" (Sayer 1999, 5).

This is not to suggest that we reject the wealth of information that can be gleaned from well-designed quantitative studies. Rather, our concern is linked to the preferential and exclusive legitimacy frequently assigned to the use of quantitative methods—methods that, when taken solely on their own merit, fail to render the complexity of the racialized cultural experience and cannot provide the analytical richness required to transform our scholarship into a truly emancipatory political project. In contrast, Latino studies scholarship needs to be independent, critical, and infused with what C. Wright Mills (2002) terms "sociological imagination"—a pedagogical and investigative discourse that provides us with an agenda of policies and practices that can assist Latino studies scholars to map out the possibilities for economic democracy and social justice, particularly in the face of neoliberal excess and scientism.

Critical Scholarship

> What we choose to emphasize in this complex history will determine our lives. (Zinn, cited in Loeb 1999)

Our discussion of Latino studies is directed toward promoting critical scholarship—scholarly work carried out with the expressed intent of challenging the structures of racialized class inequalities. This approach particularly influences how we participate in the construction of knowledge in our classrooms and as public intellectuals out in the world. As such, a critical Latino studies program must begin with a clear vision and its relationship to the ever-changing world. This is no easy task given that Latino studies is not a monolithic enterprise and that all of us work within the contested terrain of both multidisciplinary expectations and community exigencies. Nevertheless, what allows us to struggle together across our differences is the fact that social justice and economic democracy are central to the political project that first inspired the scholarly formation of the field. With this as our starting point, there are several issues that need to be consistently revisited in the course of Latino studies research. In the spirit of W. E. B. Du Bois, we need to "return to the basics" of history, political economy, and public policy in our efforts to effectively challenge racism and class inequality within institutions of higher education. Greater focus must be placed on comparative work in the field (i.e., studies that compare different racialized ethnic "Latino" groups or that compare the U.S. Latinos with Latinos in Latin American countries).[2] By so doing, we can develop knowledge not only of how we are similar but also of how we are different.

Currently, there are a variety of theoretical debates influencing both research and pedagogy within Latino studies. It is important for us to be consistently cognizant and engaged in these debates. For example, feminist theories are vital to our knowledge of Latinas and their location within our communities and the larger social context. Feminist theories are particularly important to understanding how Latinas move across contested terrain to give meaning to their racialized, gendered identities.[3] The work on Latino masculinities seeks to provide a more complex understanding of Latino men, their identities, and their subjectivities in an effort to disrupt commonly held assumptions that make homogeneous and reify the experience of Latino males within U.S. contexts.[4]

Postmodern theories, with their emphasis on fragmentation and difference, the rupture of metanarratives, and the engagement of identity politics have also influenced the way issues of culture and identity are engaged within the classroom and community. In contending with questions of "race," Latino critical race theory (LatCrit)[5] has left its mark on the field. Using this approach, legal scholars whose work represents theoretically diverse perspectives ascribe primary explanatory power to the concept of "race." Similarly, postcolonial theories, including more recently the scholarship on *Latinidad*,[6] have contributed to our understanding of human agency, the politics of location and space, and the struggle for decolonization—all key concepts in understanding the complexity and diversity of Latinos and Latinas in U.S. society.

While Latino studies is experiencing something of a renaissance within the academy, there has also been a renewed intellectual and political interest in historical materialism. Despite Latino studies scholars who impertinently deride Marxist methodology as unfashionable and obsolete, we welcome its renewal. In the past the retreat from political economy and class within African American and Latino studies scholarship was stirred by a response to the narrowness of reductionist economic arguments—and rightly so, for many early Marxist scholars tended to focus on class without paying rigorous attention to questions of racism, sexism, or heterosexism. However, today we dispute post-Marxist claims that classical Marxism hinders engagement with important issues of racialized identities and inequalities. Instead, we contend that it is not a feat of economic reductionism to treat with analytical specificity the notion of class as a relationship and as a means for examining inequalities of power and wealth in contemporary capitalism. Nor is it reductive to understand how class relations of power lead us to organize our work and political involvement in particular ways or guide our practical consideration as to the strategies we use to struggle for workers' rights, housing, education, immigration, and health care. Instead, such forms of analysis engage class as being intrinsic to all social relations and, thus, view all social arrangements as configured, dialectically, by the context of contemporary capitalist social formations.

As Latino studies scholars strive to make sense of the current political economy operating locally and globally, theories of globalization also surface in discussions of late capitalism and the rapid movement and exploitation of labor and resources, as well as the economic and political power wielded by multinational corporations.[7] However, these arguments have generated considerable debate among progressive educators and theorists. While there are those who have incorporated theories of globalization in their critiques of contemporary social problems, others argue that it is just the same old capitalism working as usual, the same old capitalism that must be fiercely challenged.[8]

This latter view seeks to reintroduce a class analysis to the construction of social theory and public policy and, in so doing, makes central its critique of capitalism. Wood (1994) explains succinctly what it means to challenge capitalism. "Addressing capitalism means considering it as a historically specific system of social relations, a social form with its own logic and its own laws of motion . . . the imperatives of competition, profit maximization, 'productivity,' 'growth' and 'flexibility' with all their social and ideological consequences" (28). Wood clearly calls for scholarship that asks how power is tied to external conditions, the social impact of changing modes of production upon workers, the political economy and its impact on class formations through the way it structures the social conditions of institutions and community life, the increasing significance of class, and the specificity of capitalism as a totalizing system of social and political domination and exploitation. In concert with this view, we argue that to ignore this dimension has far-reaching political implications for the future, particularly during a time of dramatic demographic shift.

The Changing Demographics

> Official celebratory pronouncements . . . hardly conceal diffused anxieties about the impending impact of projected demographic changes in the Latino population of the United States. (Rosaldo 1989, 214)

In January 2003, the U.S. Census Bureau estimated the Latino population to be 37 million, constituting 13 percent of the total population. With these new numbers, Latinos have the dubious distinction of being the nation's largest minority group, surpassing the estimated African American population of 36.2 million. To make sense of current conditions, we must be attentive to the impact of such changes in the regions where large Latino populations reside and what these changes mean to the local, national, and international political economy. For example, it is impossible to ignore what many are calling the "browning" or "Latinization" of vast metropolitan areas in the United States (Santa Ana 2002; Laó-Montes and Davila 2000). This phenomenon is vividly exemplified in the current population of Los Angeles County, where over 4.2 million of the 9.8 million residents are Latinos.

Population projections claim that by the year 2005, "minority" residents are expected to become the majority of the population in most large urban centers. Already in large neighborhoods of Los Angeles, New York, Chicago, Dallas, and Miami, Latino residents constitute the majority, with "the four most populous states—California, New York, Texas, and Florida—[containing] more than 60 percent of the nation's Latinos" (Gonzalez 2000, xi). But according to Jorge Mariscal (2003), this phenomenon is even beginning to occur in the Deep South where "Latino immigrants have moved in large numbers into the old confederacy" (1). Indeed, during the 1990s, the national census documented a dramatic increase in the Latino population of several Southern states.

TABLE 1

1990–2000 Percent of Increase in
Hispanic/Latino Population in Southern States

State	Percent
North Carolina	323.9
Arkansas	323.3
Georgia	299.6
Tennessee	278.2

Source: U.S. Census, 2000.

In order to understand the evolving public needs of these cities it is important to recognize the migratory patterns that give rise to the shifting landscape of many working-class Latino neighborhoods. For example, more than 50 percent of all Latinos in California are foreign-born, over 700,000 of them in Central America. The significance of this statistic cannot be downplayed, since many have come to California in response to regional wars and impoverishment spurred on by historical and contemporary U.S. foreign economic policies in Latin America. The growing number of diverse Latino immigrants poses a positive challenge to our scholarship and pedagogy, pushing against the grain of traditionally defined notions of Latino identity—from the more obvious political concerns about how we label Latino populations to the more complex issue of redefining ideas of citizenship (Oboler 1995).

We maintain that complex ideas such as citizenship are contested concepts, precisely because they are related to wider cultural and social issues of racialized class identities.[9] Such issues have often been sidelined or neglected within the context of research on and practices of Latino identity politics. Much of this research has failed to engage the complexity of histories, cultures, and regional economies that shape the construction of diverse Latino identities.[10] This is well illustrated by many U.S.-born and immigrant Latinos who not only identify with indigenous or *mestizo* roots, but who identify themselves as Afro-Latinos. This complexity was clearly evident in the 2000 census, which asked Latinos to claim a particular "racial origin." "Some of the nation's 35 million Latinos scribbled in the margins that they were Aztec or Mayan. A fraction said they were Indian. Nearly 48 percent described themselves as white and two percent described themselves as black. Fully 42 percent said they were 'some other race'" (Fears 2002, A1). Such accounts clearly point to the need to pay careful analytical attention to racialized constructions of identity in these times of major demographic shifts, changing class formations, and new forms of global dislocation. One-size-fits-all responses to Latino education, citizenship, and well-being within the United States will always be insufficient.

The Limits of Identity Politics

> We work with raced identities on already reified ground. In the context of domination, raced identities are imposed and internalized, then renegotiated and reproduced. From artificial to natural, we court a hard-to-perceive social logic that reproduces *the very conditions we strain to overcome.* (Cruz 1996, 35; emphasis in original)

Since the 1960s, Latino studies scholars have tended overwhelmingly to focus on notions of "race" in ways that draw directly on the intellectual and political tradition of many African American scholars. Hence, the use of the concept of "race" became the new orthodoxy among Chicano scholars. In an effort to reconceptualize the study of Chicanos in the United States, an approach was developed that established "race" (and later class) as a primary analytical category (Barrera 1979). This new formulation quickly took shape within the humanities and social sciences, as a variety of models emerged. One such model was "internal colonialism" which discussed Chicanos as a colonized "racial" group in much the same way as many radical scholars theorized the African American condition within the U.S. political economy.[11] The obvious strength of this model (or perhaps better described as a metaphor) was the importance given to racial dynamics in shaping the cultural and socioeconomic conditions of Chicanos.[12] Protected by the force of cultural nationalist rhetoric, class was "increasingly displaced by concerns for race" (Dunn 1998, 22). As such, association of the term "race" with power, resistance, and self-determination has veiled the problematics of "race" as a social construct, while "race" as an analytical term has remained a "paper tiger"—seemingly powerful in terms of discourse but ineffectual as an analytical metaphor—incapable of moving us away from the pervasive notion of "race" as an innate determinant of behavior.

Consequently, much of the past literature on Latino populations, with its emphasis on such issues as "racial inequality," "racial segregation," "racial identity," and "racial consciousness," has utilized "race" as a central category of analysis for interpreting the social conditions of inequality and marginalization. In turn, this literature has reinforced a racialized politics of identity and representation, with its problematic emphasis on "racial" identity as the overwhelming impulse for political action (Darder and Torres 1999). Thus, identity politics has become the battlefield for efforts to construct a coherent social movement among Latinos in the United States.[13]

Unfortunately, the reliance on political identity notions of "race" and representation to theorize conditions of racialization has seriously obscured the imperatives of capitalist accumulation and the impact of class divisions within Latino communities. Wood (1994) critiques the folly of this position, exposing the limitations of an identity politics that fails to contend with the fact that capitalism is the most totalizing system of social relations the world has ever known. The result of theoretical interventions based on identity politics has been the conspicuous absence of a systematic analysis of class relations and critique of capitalism in much of the work on Latino, African American, Native American, and Asian populations.

Ramon Grosfoguel and Chloe S. Georas (1996) posit that "social identities are constructed and reproduced in complex and entangled political, economic, and symbolic hierarchy" (193). Given this complex entanglement, what we need is a more dynamic and fluid notion of the way we think about different cultural identities in the context of contemporary capitalist social formations. Such a perspective of identity would support our efforts to shatter static and frozen notions that perpetuate ahistorical, apolitical, and classless views of culturally pluralistic societies, particularly as it relates to the experiences of racialized groups. How we analytically accomplish this is no easy matter. But, however this task is approached, we must not "confuse respect for the plurality of human experience and social struggles with a complete dissolution of historical causality, where there is nothing but diversity, difference and contingency, no unifying structures, no logic of process, no capitalism and therefore no negation of it, no universal project of human emancipation" (Wood 1995, 263).

In a seminal study of Mexican Americans and Puerto Ricans in Chicago, Felix Padilla (1985) concluded that it was the shared experience of structural conditions of inequalities (i.e., substandard housing, poor education, and menial employment) that provided a basis for establishing identity and building social consciousness, rather than a pre-existing, essentialized identity as Latinos. In considering the implication of Padilla's study, particularly with respect to Latino identity in the context of the global economy, the shattering of nationalist barriers, and the process of racialization, Martha Gimenez (1999) suggests,

> Perhaps it will be the historical role of Latino workers . . . to break the limits of identity politics by reclaiming all the determinants of their identities; not just their culture, their language, their historical heritage, and their current selective understandings of their traditions and sense of who they are, but also their class location and their understanding of themselves as workers who with their labor and the labor of their children are making this nation what it is (179).

Hence, if we are to effectively challenge the destructive economic impact of globalization on Latino and other racialized populations, we argue that a politics of identity is grossly inept and unsuited for building and sustaining collective political movements that can effectively challenge the structures of social exclusion and economic inequality. Instead, we need to critically reframe the very terrain that gives life to our political understanding of what it means to struggle against widening class differentiation and ever-increasing racialized inequality. Through an analytical process of reframing, we can expand the terms by which Latino identities are considered, examined, and defined, recognizing that racialized relations of power are inherently shaped by the profound organizational and spatial transformations of the capitalist economy.

Class Matters

> One of the main reasons for studying class structure is because of
> its importance in explaining other elements of class analysis, espe-
> cially class formation, class consciousness and class struggle.
> (Wright 1997, 41)

Central to our comprehension of pedagogy and research in Latino studies is our ability to engage class not as an identity or a phenomenon equal
to other forms of oppression, but rather as relations of power that encompass social processes that reproduce structural inequality. From this
standpoint, we can consider how the relationships among culture, class,
power, and ideology impact the construction of knowledge; how we
might move toward dismantling the structures of racialized inequality
which persist in society today, as opposed to reform efforts; and how we
contend with political efforts to completely dismantle the remnants of
progressive health, education, and welfare policies.

As noted in chapter 1, the collapse of the Soviet Union in the 1980s, in
conjunction with the shift toward postmodern paradigms of knowledge
and theoretical orientations, resulted in a retreat from class analysis.
Latino studies was no exception. We are well aware that some people may
see our assertion of the importance of class analysis in Latino studies scholarship as a return to an outdated theoretical paradigm. But Marxist theory
has always been a site of conflicting and competing perspectives. Moreover, our concern with the question of class analysis goes far beyond simple ideological contestation. For us, class is tied intrinsically to material
conditions in society and to our understanding of the way relations of production and asymmetrical structures of power shape daily life in very concrete ways. For example, there is no doubt that large numbers of African
American, Latino, and Native American workers fail to ever find long-
term or substantial employment in the labor market. In fact, Latino and
other racialized minorities are disproportionately represented in low-income jobs and state unemployment rolls. And an interrelationship clearly
exists between Latin American migration to the United States and exclusionary processes which ensure that the ranks of the small entrepreneur include Latino immigrants who sustain a complex of financial and cultural
ties with their countries of origin. These are but two simple examples that
speak to the significance of class in our understanding of the structural
conditions and social realities that impact Latino communities today.

A class analysis must also be central to our efforts to better understand Latino communities and issues of education, or else we risk reinscribing existing inequities pertaining to educational attainment and achievement opportunities. For example, the digital divide in the United States is no longer concerned primarily with describing inequitable physical access to computers at school for certain marginalized, low-income groups, but rather, is increasingly used to describe inequitable differences in quality of new technology use in schools (Cuban 2001). As we move from living and working in an industrial to a "postindustrial" society, fundamental questions remain to be answered about the "proper" relationship between education, work, and new technologies. These include questions such as: Which groups have the most ready access to effective uses of new technology in schools, and why? What is (or what should be) the emancipatory role of technology in schools, colleges, and universities (i.e., distance learning, flexible course offerings, small-scale and large-scale activism, and access to vital information)? What are the consequences of technology-rich education in relation to Latino students' social and academic development in particular, when these students have historically had far less access to new technologies than their white or Asian counterparts (Tornatzky, Macias, and Jones 2002), especially within the context of high-stakes testing and accountability-driven remediation of Latino students' standard English literacy? What social and moral values does technology-driven education cultivate, and what might this mean for current and future conceptions of and practices associated with "being a good citizen" for Latino students enrolled in U.S. public schools?

To engage such questions effectively requires that we recognize that class and "race" are concepts of a different sociological order. Class and "race" do not occupy the same analytical space and thus cannot constitute explanatory alternatives to one another. Class is a material space, even within the mainstream definition that links the concept to occupation, income status, and educational attainment—all of which reflect the materiality of class, though without analytical specificity. Hence, class can only be rigorously analyzed by recognizing that the social relations of production are germane to any social justice or emancipatory political project.

By posing critical questions that interrogate the power relations that condition and structure the nature and extent of exploitation across classes, Latino studies scholars can unveil the internal organization and social relations at work between contending classes. In the final analysis, the relationship between appropriators and producers rests on the relative strength of classes and the way these are thrust into the political arena of class struggle (Wood 1995). True to this view, we challenge the post-Marxist dismissal of class as an analytical category and, instead, reaffirm class analysis in Latino studies research and pedagogy as essential in the face of staggering economic inequality.

Inequality in the "New Economy"

> We are all living through an unprecedented situation marked by dramatic new developments, including not only the New Economy boom and bust, but also an unheard of polarization of wealth . . . a phenomenon of capital accumulation and crisis—hence class struggle. (Sweezy and Magdoff 2001, 15)[14]

Angel Gonzalez of the *Dallas Morning News* reported on December 29, 2003, that the purchasing power of Latinos in 2003 was estimated to be $586 billion. By 2010 it is expected to reach $1 trillion. This hype of Latino success obfuscates a more serious and long-lasting structural problem that is occurring within a larger context of growing class inequality and downsizing in corporate America.[15] The growing gap between rich and poor is one of the United States's most compelling issues, particularly when we consider the overwhelming concentration of wealth and income that remains in the hands of a few. In spite of this, it is commonplace for educators to consider questions of pedagogy without addressing fundamental social questions related to economic inequality. Yet we cannot gain a better understanding of what is driving many of the difficulties Latinos are facing in this country today without addressing the changing nature of the capitalist economy. These problems must be set within the political-economic sphere of the state and capitalist society. By grounding our work in material concerns, we are intellectually and politically motivated to consider, at the very least, such questions as: Who is working? Who is not? Who is gaining economic ground? Who is losing ground?

It is imperative that Latino studies scholars investigate more seriously changing conditions of labor and the consequences of "globalization." In so doing, we must recognize that there is considerable theoretical debate over how best to describe the changing nature of work and the direction of the modern capitalist economy. Competing opinions abound as to the extent and meaning of these changes and whether they represent a new kind of epochal shift in the basic logic of capitalist accumulation. Once again, the city of Los Angeles can provide a worthy illustration of this particular issue.

As a consequence of the deindustrialization of Los Angeles, thousands of workers have experienced, first-hand, what it means to see work disappear and to contend with the accompanying structural conditions that have created deep-seated class divisions in the region. As a direct outcome, unemployment in Los Angeles was higher at the end of the twentieth century than it was in 1969 (Scott and Soja 1996). Similarly, these conditions have had a perilous effect on the city's diverse populations. Again, we turn to the 1992 unrest in South Central Los Angeles, which contrary to its portrayal by the media and many academics, resulted largely from high rates of joblessness, rather than from issues of "race relations." In fact, over 60 percent of those arrested were Latinos. By characterizing this event as a crisis in "race relations"—first, between blacks and Koreans, then between blacks and Latinos, and finally back to blacks and whites—the media both avoided and prevented any substantive inquiry into the structural economic problems of the city and region. Moreover, the interpretation of the riots as a "race relations" problem failed to take into account the drastic shifts in demographic patterns which have created new dynamics of class and racialized relations in Los Angeles (Valle and Torres 2000)—urban dynamics intricately tied to "the globalizing pressure of capitalism to abandon the will to social investment within the national-domestic sphere" (Cruz 1996, 29).

This perspective is further sustained by an analysis of the problems inherent in contemporary capitalist restructuring. The reindustrialization of large urban centers with light manufacturing, for example, represents an urban development strategy that is partly responsible for stagnant wages, given the abundance of surplus labor owing to increasing rates of unemployment and cheap immigrant labor. Undoubtedly, this has contributed to the further economic decline of many working-class neighborhoods in the large and densely populated inner cities. Similarly, the closing of heavy manufacturing production plants (such as automotive and aerospace factories) across the nation has had a deleterious effect on Latino and African American workers in particular. Such closures, along with the negative repercussions of NAFTA on workers, have contributed to the phenomenon discussed openly by even the right—the dismantling of the middle class and the increasing polarization of wealth. In addition, the economic instability of many working-class Latino communities has been further exacerbated by the replacement of union labor by nonunion labor and the reduction of benefits and real wages during the 1990s (Darder and Torres 1997).

Although these conditions are tremendously detrimental to the quality of life for Latino populations in the United States, Latino studies scholars must also take note of positive grassroots efforts to strike back at the ravages of deepening economic inequality. For example, recent neighborhood efforts in Latino communities have resulted in the introduction and passage of Living Wage ordinances. Latino youth involved with *Californians for Justice* and *Schools Not Jails* have been instrumental to community organizing campaigns for democratic schooling. Such communitywide efforts represent a significant and tangible implementation of structural reforms at the local level, efforts that can only be successful when structural inequalities are intricately linked with the process of racialization.

From Race to Racialization

> For three hundred years black Americans insisted that "race" was not a usefully distinguishing factor in human relationships. During those same three centuries every academic discipline . . . insisted that "race" was the determining factor in human development.
> (Morrison 1989, 3)

Everywhere we look, policy pundits, journalists, and academics alike continue to work within categories of "race" as though there is consensus regarding their meaning and analytical significance. Like all other components of what Gramsci (1971) called "common sense," much of the everyday usage of "race" is uncritical. This phenomenon, of course, is no different for Latino populations. Yet some would argue that Latinos relate to the issue of "race" with more fluidity than do other racialized groups, transcending "the binary divisions adopted in the United States" (Rodriguez 2000, 123). This is reflected in the various terms used to describe a person through the signification of their skin color (i.e., *mestizo, morena, trigueño,* and *mulata,* among others). However, this fluidity, albeit a legacy of Spanish colonization and carefully constructed social and exclusionary hierarchies of status, is not reflected in U.S. bureaucratic structures. Hence, it is not unusual to find that dark-skinned Latino immigrants from Brazil, Colombia, Panama, and other Latin American countries are surprised to learn that they are categorized as black within the context of the U.S. racialized gaze.

There are those who might conclude, "race matters in Latin America, but it matters differently" (Fears 2002, A1). This may well be related to the historical fact that, until recently, questions of class have foregrounded liberatory struggles, despite the fact that racism has been at work in all Latin American countries. In simplest terms, this is reflected by the typically light-skinned phenotypical characteristics of the elite class, as compared with the generally darker-skinned features of most members from poor and working-class populations. So, although Latino immigrants may engage the notion of race differently, there is no question but that their perceptions are, nevertheless, linked to the particular processes of racialization inherent in the histories of Latin American conquest and slavery in their countries of origin.[16]

In these times, we would be hard-pressed to find scholars who would subscribe openly to the use of "race" as a determinant of any specific social phenomenon associated with inherent genetic characteristics. In 1997 the American Anthropological Association recommended that the U.S. government scrap the term "race" on official forms, since it had no scientific justification in human biology. Recent human genome research supports the fact that "race" has no biological foundation. However, such events have done little to challenge or erase the disturbing "scientific" assertion—that "race" determines academic success—made by Herrnstein and Murray (1994) in *The Bell Curve* or the "cultural group" essentialism of Abigail and Stephan Thernstrom (2003) in *No Excuses: Closing the Racial Gap in Learning*. These works illustrate the theoretical minefield of perpetuating "race" as an analytical category in the social sciences and the potential negative consequences on racialized groups. In these instances, the use of the term "race" serves to conceal the truth, that it is not "race" that determines academic success, but rather the deeply entrenched exclusionary forces within schools and society that sustain educational inequality. It is within the historical and contemporary context of such scholarship that differences in skin color are signified as marks suggesting the existence of different "races."

The political appeal and continued academic currency (across the ideological spectrum) of the concept of "race" within the social sciences and humanities is seriously challenged in this volume. We reject its use as a discursive tool ("race" as discourse) as well as its so-called objective use as a commonsense classification of human populations. We are aware that our position that "race" is a fiction is bound to be seen by many activists and scholars as the endorsement of a color-blind view or, as Silvio Torres-Saillant (2003) argues, "an elusive cutting edge rather than from a down to earth assessment of what has worked in the overall effort to elevate the condition of ethnic minority groups" (133).

This, however, is not what we are arguing. Our work in no way seeks to refute the past political accomplishments of racialized ethnic groups. However, we do firmly contend that doing without the fiction of "race" will not strip us of our political and symbolic agency. Rather, a reconceptualization from "race" to racism will add specificity to our struggle and provide the necessary ideological context to engage the structures of inequalities in a capitalist society. Moreover, we recognize that past attempts to remedy the impact of racism have fallen short and, as such, we must carefully, but boldly, examine the weaknesses in approaches to scholarship and politics that would prefer to mark "race" as the central category of interrogation and struggle, rather than the capitalist economy and its inseparable relationship to racism (Miles and Brown 2003).

As we have repeatedly argued, the fixation on skin color is a product of signification, rather than a product of some "truth" concerning an essential relationship between skin color and inherent group abilities or collective destiny. People identify skin color as marking or symbolizing other phenomena in a variety of social contexts in which other significations occur. When social practices include or exclude people in light of the signification of skin color, collective identities are produced and social inequalities are structured (Miles and Torres 1999). If "race matters," it matters only because of the significance we attach to phenotypical differences. From our point of view, it is the economic and ideological basis of capitalism and the social relations of racialized inequalities (not "race") that have built the empire of capital. And it is the interrogation of these categories that must be at the heart of critical scholarship and political efforts focused on the amelioration of human suffering.

Hence, to interpret more lucidly the conditions faced by Latino populations requires us to move beyond the idea of "race" to an understanding of racialization and its impact on class formations. To continue using the concept of "race" as an analytic term is to affix and essentialize skin color characteristics in relation to certain groups and elide the processes involved in the social construction of "race." The former offers no hope of change or reform (i.e., skin color is something to be "worked around") while the latter is far more dynamic, in that it offers ways of challenging categories that undermine the agency of marginalized groups. The concept of racism thus marks a bold analytical transition from the language of "race" by recognizing the centrality of racism and the process of racialization in our understanding of exclusionary practices that give rise to structural inequalities.

Because social theories of racism are predominantly anchored in a black-white paradigm of "race relations," those in Latino studies are severely limited in their efforts to speak to the complexity of Latino racialization. One of the most limiting aspects of the black-white framework is its tendency to obstruct or camouflage the need to examine particular histories and contextual dimensions that give rise to different forms of racism around the globe. The subsequent conflation of racialized relations into a black-white paradigm has often rendered Latino populations invisible or relegated them to the status of "second-class oppression." This has prevented Latino studies scholars from focusing on significant differences among Latino populations and from delving more fully into comparative histories of racism and seeing how these are linked to class inequalities.

If we are to grasp the complexity of contemporary Latino life, the racialized language of "black" and "white" must be dispensed with and replaced by a new conceptual language rooted in, but not determined by, the political economy of labor migration and capitalist social and class relations.[17] Mariscal (2003) alludes to this need with respect to Latino immigrant workers in the deep South, where demographic changes reflect the historical nature of the racialization process.

> They have little knowledge of the struggles for equal rights and the history of anti-Mexican racism in the Southwest. As they enter a culture based on black/white relations, these workers are unaware of regional histories, past labor struggles and the persistence of long-standing "southern values." In effect, they walk into a black/white universe like virtual aliens from another planet. (1)

Further, Mariscal suggests that the recent media coverage of the Trent Lott affair illustrates that the discussion of race in this country "is still firmly grounded in a narrow and antiquated black/white reality" (1).

Toward a Critical Theory of Racism

> The idea of "race" has profound meanings in the everyday world, but these have no scientific credibility and I can therefore find no reason why those who write in the Marxist tradition should wish to legitimise an ideological notion by elevating it to a central analytical position. (Miles 1984, 232)

Recent structural changes in the U.S. political economy and increasing diversity within Latino communities have made the issue of racism more complex than ever before. But rather than occupying a central position, these historical socioeconomic changes have served merely as a backdrop to the contemporary theoretical debates on the meaning of "race" and representation in the United States today—debates often founded on deeply psychologized or abstracted notions of racialized differences and conflicts. This constitutes a significant bone of contention, generating many unanswered questions regarding the continued use of the idea of race in theorizing the Latino life condition: What does it mean to utilize "race" in light of the growing complexities we are facing within both the social and political arenas? What are the strengths and limitations of a "race-centered" politics? How is racism structured within the context of advanced capitalist relations of power?

Such inquiry into the analytical utility of "race" in Latino studies scholarship is by no means meant to negate the worthiness of ongoing work on racialized inequalities or to obstruct the struggle against racism or deny that "race" is a social construction. Rather, it represents an effort to seek greater analytical clarity in the way we make sense of cultural, historical, and political differences. Moreover, we need to critically expose, with greater specificity, the way the ideology of racism produces notions of "race," as opposed to the popular belief that the existence of "races" produces racism.

This discussion highlights the need for Latino studies scholars to interrogate with greater analytical depth the terms we use and the concepts we commonly uphold. For example, it is not uncommon to find the words "race" and "culture" being used interchangeably in discussions of Chicanos, Puerto Ricans, and other Latino populations. Instead of linking the notion of culture to class relations that emerge at the point of production (or social relations of production), most scholars link culture to the notion of "race"—a concept associated with phenotypical traits but now linked to the notion of social construction, shared histories, and narratives categorized within the racialized category of Latino.

Meanwhile, the common practice of framing social relations as "race relations" continues to obscure material conditions of inequality. This is exemplified by educational theories that assign significance to "racial" characteristics, rather than attributing student responses to school conditions, historically shaped by structural inequalities that determine the context in which students must achieve. This conspicuous absence of class analysis veils the actual reasons why so many Latino, African American, and other racialized students fare poorly on standardized tests, are overrepresented in remedial programs, and continue to drop out of high schools and universities at alarming rates. Accordingly, educational solutions are often derived from distorted perceptions of the problem and lead to misguided policies and practices.

The politics of busing in the early 1970s provides an excellent example of this phenomenon of distortion. Social scientists studying "race relations" concluded that contact among "black" and "white" students would decrease the incidence of prejudice and that the educational conditions of "black" students would improve if they were bused to "white" schools outside their neighborhoods. More than thirty years later, there are many Latino and African American parents and educators who adamantly condemn the busing solution (a solution based on a discourse of "race") as not only fundamentally destructive to the fabric of African American and Latino communities, but also an erroneous social experiment that improved neither the academic performance of minority students nor the economic well-being of racialized communities.

This example illustrates how racialized constructs of culture can obscure or overshadow social arrangements of inequality intrinsic to class relations, including those premised on racism. Concealing this fact makes it more difficult to address effectively the motivating forces for the construction of particular social arrangements, whether these are marked by physical, geographical, or ideological signifiers. Hence, an interrogation of the use of "race" is tremendously important within Latino studies, given that nothing occurs without implicating the material conditions that shape the way individuals and groups locate themselves within the context of the larger society.

Yet we recognize that mere efforts to undo and eliminate the "race" as an analytical category in our scholarship will so little to remove its use from the popular imagination and the discourse of everyday life. Moreover, in a country like the United States, which is filled with historical examples of exploitation, violence, and murderous acts justified by both popular opinions and scientific ideas of "race," it is next to impossible to convince people that "race" does not exist as a "natural" category. So in the words of Guillaumin (1995), "Let us be clear about this. The idea of race is a technical means, a machine for committing murder. And its effectiveness is not in doubt" (107). While "races" do not exist, what does exist is the tenacious and unrelenting idea of "race" that fuels the ravages of racism worldwide.

Future struggles against the devastations of racism and capitalism must at long last contend with the reality that there are no "races" and therefore no "race relations." In light of this view, we call for a critical reconceptualization of racism with which to analyze the historical and contemporary social experiences and institutional realities faced by Latino communities and other racialized populations. Insofar as such a concept, whether employed in social investigation or political struggle, reveals patterns of discrimination and resulting inequalities, it can also help us grapple more specifically with those actions that must be taken to dismantle the structural inequalities we encounter in our everyday lives. Such a critical theory of racism represents a bold and forthright move to challenge commonsense notions of "race" that often not only lead to profound forms of essentialism and ahistorical perceptions of oppression, but also make it nearly impossible to dismantle the external material structures of exploitation and domination that sustain racialized inequalities within the body politic of the capitalist state.

The Nature of the Capitalist State

> A theory of the state is always a theory of society and of the distribution of power in that society. (Miliband 1969, 2)

The nature of the capitalist state is another important issue often ignored in Latino studies scholarship. This is a serious omission when we consider current material conditions of contemporary society. The state has been seized and "democracy" has been effectively subverted.[18] Politicians, media barons, judges, powerful corporate lobbies, and government officials are imbricated in an elaborate underhand configuration that completely undermines the lateral arrangement of "checks and balances" (Roy 2003, 7). Accordingly, state policies of deregulation and the free market have prevailed and, as Arundhati Roy (2003) asserts, neoliberal capitalists

> have mastered the techniques of infiltrating the instruments of democracy—the "independent" judiciary, the "free press," the [government]—molding them to their purpose. The project of corporate globalization has cracked the code. Free elections, a free press, and an independent judiciary mean little when the free market has reduced them to commodities on sale to the highest bidder (6).

Driven by corporate forces, state policies have ushered in devastating welfare cutbacks, corporate corruption, economic foreign treaties, the war in Afghanistan, "homeland security," and in 2003 the war on Iraq. These events fueled the anti-intellectual fervor of the popular media while skewing popular opinion away from any meaningful critique of capitalist interests. In the midst of these events, there was scant news coverage of the atrocities of U.S. oil companies in Nigeria, the unabashed sale of obsolete U.S. weapons to impoverished nations, or the United States's role in the creation of instability and unrest in the Middle East and other parts of the globe. And as Juan Gonzalez reminds us, "compared to the barrage of media attention that accompanied the original debate over NAFTA, most news outlets have ignored the horrendous aftermath" (Gonzalez 2000, 245).

With the unbridled ferment and advancement of capital, the safety net of the welfare state is quickly being eroded. As conservative interests channel massive expenditures toward the military and prison-industrial complex, support for health, education, and housing for the poor continues to wane in comparison. In 2003 the projections for California's budget reflected this unfortunate trend in the distribution of public expenditures. The yearly allocation for state prisons was the only line item in the budget to increase for 2004. In addition, popular conservative campaigns since the 1980s have also done their part to destroy the power of unions, abolish immigrant rights, privatize education and health services, eradicate affirmative action, and dismantle bilingual education.

How, then, do we understand the nature and impact of such state policies and campaigns upon Latino populations? In our view, we must make our scholarship and pedagogy analytically more rigorous so as to better understand how state policies and practices have historically functioned to reproduce inequalities. In so doing, we need to keep in mind that "empirical observation must in each separate instance bring out empirically and without any mystification and speculation, the connection of the social and political structure with production" (Marx and Engels 1970, 46). Such critical analysis of the capitalist state and its class structure, while conspicuously absent in much of the research in Latino studies, is found in Marxist-inspired works by scholars such as Mario Barrera (1979) and Gilbert Gonzalez and Raul Fernandez (2003). In Barrera's seminal volume, *Race and Class in the Southwest*, for example, he provides a formidable class analysis of racialized class inequality and the positioning of the capitalist state in Chicano economic history.

The nature of the state must be fully interrogated as a site of conflict and counterhegemonic struggle. The questions that must be engaged include: What is the role of the capitalist state in the reproduction of inequality? To what extent are racialized relations autonomous from state-structured economic relations? In what ways are class, gender, and racialized relations structured by state policies? How do class, gender, and racialized relations structure each other? Research on the accumulation and legitimation needs of the capitalist state[19] can provide needed clarity in understanding Latino conditions of racialized class inequality. Such research can also point to the kinds of public policies that could restructure conditions of social and economic exploitation in a liberal capitalist democracy.

Critical Policy Studies

> The promise of the social sciences is to bring reason to bear on human affairs. (Mills 2002, 192)

More than ever, issues of pedagogy and research in Latino studies need to be addressed with respect to public policy and the conditions of everyday life. It is disheartening to find that Latino studies scholars often ignore, in both their teaching and research, the particulars of public policy and its impact on communities. Even when policy is engaged, scholars often lack specificity and rigor in their theoretical understanding of what constitutes public policy. To address both these concerns we must move away from the quantitative policy interventions that have historically been highly technical and grounded in normative political science.

In response, there are those in the field of Latino studies who advance the human capital model in public policy recommendations as a solution to structural inequalities. However, this model of analysis provides only a narrow view of production and an even more limited understanding of social reproduction in the political economy. Left to its own devices, the human capital model can inadvertently lead to victim-blaming interpretations in which Latinos are ultimately held responsible for institutional failures to provide adequate schooling, job opportunities, and optimal health care within their communities.

Instead, we believe that critical policy approaches to class and structural analysis provide a better means of comprehending and transforming the social and economic inequalities faced by Latinos today. From this perspective, income inequalities result from the normal operation of the capitalist economy. That is, income inequality is a structural aspect of the capitalist economy and does not derive from individual differences in skills and competencies. More importantly, class is defined by the social relations of production, which gives it a central role in mediating income inequalities in U.S. society.

For years, expectations of social change were founded on the possibility of litigation to correct social wrongs. But today, the terrain of social change is shifting, as the role of litigation in social change seems to be declining while that of public policy is increasing. This is particularly evident in states like California, where the initiative process seems to have run amuck[20] and litigation is too slow a process to counter the wave of right-wing corporate interests that dominate the political scene—especially in the context of education. Thus, fifty years after the monumental victory in *Brown v. Board of Education*, it is strikingly evident that the traditional approach to public policy cannot effectively address racialized, gendered, and class inequalities.

Public policy, formulated around political sound bites and tied merely to number crunching or limited personalized accounts, has failed to provide Latino scholars and activists with the necessary mechanisms to dismantle the pervasive structures of inequality. There is a dire need for engagement not only with the technical dimensions of public policy (i.e., initiatives, referendums, and the ballot box) but also with the conceptual ideological apparatus of public policy. This requires us to question more deeply the philosophical dimensions and political interests that undergird public policy discourse. It also demands that our work focus on "the things people see everyday, around issues that touch people's daily lives, like health and work, the environment and housing, and the education of their children" (Marable 1998, 2).

For these reasons, our work must not remain hidden within the safety of the classroom nor be invisible and limited to the realm of policy discourse. We need a proactive approach to public policy within the field of Latino studies—one that advances empirically rich and theoretically bold policy alternatives. Here, we are guided by French sociologist Andre Gorz's (1968) notion of "non-reformist reforms"—that is, policy changes that bestow greater power and democratic rights to workers in their daily lives. By combining our pedagogy, research, and activism, Latino studies scholars can begin to draw up alternative city, state, and federal budgets that target health, education, and welfare spending. In so doing, our scholarship can be widely used to help lay out alternative strategies that support the practice of anticorporate and democratic social action. Such efforts are not meant to primarily serve the interests of policy makers and government agencies, but rather to support independent and critical research in Latino studies that scrutinizes policy in relation to its actual consequences for equality, social justice, and economic democracy.

Although we are very cognizant that policy memos alone will not create a new politics of social change or democratic renewal, we do need scholarship that is tied to a moral imperative of policy and social reconstruction. Public policy initiatives that are grounded in social movements and the changing class realities of Latino communities are urgently needed. However, such a daunting task cannot be accomplished without working together to build coalitions (Valle and Torres 2000; Wilson 1999). In practice, this requires us to become more creative about how we utilize both institutional and community resources. In addition, we must acknowledge the existence of racialized class divisions within our communities in order to advance and support greater democratic participation in public policy debates.

All this is to argue that we must participate more openly in the arena of public policy in order to challenge the policy pundits and political sycophants who exploit and repress community political development. In an age where urban legends, public relations schemes, and manufactured perceptions can often yield greater currency than the facts, there is an urgent need for critical scholars in Latino studies to speak truth to power. This implies a willingness to use our academic pursuits in ways that publicly expose the corrupt corporate politics of urban development, the contradictions of labor leadership, the racialized policies and practices of public education, the inhumanity of the prison-industrial complex, the atrocities of war, and other obstructions to democratic life.

In a world that is becoming fiercely polarized, Latino studies scholars must use their influence to establish and participate in policy forums that support dialogue between people in labor, education, community organizing, religion, health care, and public office. Here again, the community must serve as an indispensable site for the construction of knowledge and political action upon which we can anchor our theoretical endeavors to the actual events and conditions we find in the world. By connecting our teaching practice and research to a larger social democratic project, the classroom becomes a workplace for both professors and students. In so doing, we can expand our influence in the field in ways that can effectively contribute to our struggle against racism and economic injustice, while we infuse our pedagogy and scholarship with individual passion, political commitment, and sociological imagination.

Notes

NOTES TO INTRODUCTION

1. For a thoughtful critique of the concept of racialization, see Rohit Barot and John Bird (2001), "Racialization: The Genealogy and Critique of a Concept," in *Ethnic and Racial Studies* 24 (4) (4 July): 601–18.

2. In December 2001, Enron, the transnational energy giant with $62 billion in assets, filed the largest bankruptcy in U.S. corporate history. Enron, the seventh-largest U.S. company, employing 21,000 workers in more than forty countries, lied about its profits and stands accused of a variety of shady investment dealings and concealments of debt through false accounting. The financial scandal, in which the life savings and retirement funds of tens of thousands of workers vanished while Enron executives lined their pockets, came to the public's attention when the company's link with President George W. Bush and Vice President Dick Cheney, among other Washington officials was publicly unveiled—Enron contributed millions of dollars to finance the 2004 Bush-Cheney presidential re-election campaign. Enron's deep financial roots on Capitol Hill served to insulate the company from government attempts to regulate its business dealings.

NOTES TO CHAPTER 1

This chapter is a slightly revised version of the original essay published in Vered Amit-Talai and Caroline Knowles, eds., *Re-Situating Identities: The Politics of Race, Ethnicity, and Culture* (1996). It is printed here by permission of Broadview Press.

1. William Julius Wilson has received a great deal of criticism for his insistence on focusing on the increasing significance of class, rather than "race," in forging an understanding of the complexities of poverty within African American communities. Although we do not share Wilson's Weberian class analysis, we do agree that class divisions and class inequalities are as fundamental as they have ever been. But, unlike many critics of Wilson (see, e.g., Howard Winant 2000, 169–85), we recognize that his call for a class-based analysis (albeit a non-Marxist one) is not a dismissal of racism but a rigorous attempt at mapping

racialized inequalities within the context of a changing political economy. But we take a different normative approach to our analysis of racialized inequalities and the growing class divide—a method that allows us to treat with specificity the dialectic between the means of production and the process of racialization. For a thoughtful summary of class theory and Marxist versus Weberian class analysis see Erik Olin Wright's (1997) *Class Counts*.

2. For a thoughtful review of David Theo Goldberg's approach to race and racism, see Rose Gann's (2003) "Race, Politics, and the Racial State."

3. We find Goldberg's conceptualization of class—as merely a feature of identity—is seriously problematic. As we advance in this book, class and classes are defined in terms of a common structural position within the social organization of production (Lenin 1947). So although Goldberg does not reject class outright, he treats class in a superficial manner and employs the concept with no analytical specificity. For Goldberg, class remains outside the social relations of production and thus becomes much like other social and "racial" identities. We will return to these concerns of class, class struggle, and racism in the following chapters.

4. It should be noted, however, that in his 2002 edition of *There Ain't No Black in the Union Jack*, Paul Gilroy recants his earlier position that "race should be accorded an equivalent epistemological weight and power to shape events, structures and political patterns as other dimensions of inequality and hierarchy like class and gender" (xxvii). Further, he goes on to say that this earlier position was expressed at a time of considerable political and theoretical debate surrounding the utility of Marxist approaches to "race" and racism. He admits, "This part of the book has not endured. Its arguments for taking 'race' seriously are uncontroversial in a climate where it is likely to be taken too seriously, while racism is not taken seriously enough" (xxvii).

5. Omi and Winant refer to this as a distinction between racial awareness and racial essentialism. Compare Omi and Winant 1994, 71, with Miles 1989, 73–84.

6. See also Omi and Winant 1994, 73, and compare with Miles 1989, 57–60. See also Miles 1993 for a further discussion of historically specific racisms.

7. Post-Fordism refers to the notion that modern industrial production has moved from mass production in huge factories and with protected national markets, as pioneered by Henry Ford, toward specialized markets based on small flexible manufacturing units that are heavily invested in global competition. As a consequence of complex changes, there have been major shifts in the labor market, worker policies, and the politics of unionization. The main driving forces behind the emergence of Post-Fordism include new technologies, internationalization of capital, and the redefinition of the primary economic functions of the state. For a more in-depth discussion of Post-Fordism, see Bob Jessop's (1991) article "Post-Fordism and the State," in Ash Amin, ed., *Post-Fordism: A Reader*.

This chapter is reprinted from Marta López-Garza and David R. Diaz, eds., *Asian and Latino Immigration in a Restructuring Economy* (2001), © 2001 by the Board of Trustees of the Leland Stanford Jr. University, by permission of the publisher.

1. Young Suk Lee is the pseudonym of an actual retailer in the garment district in Los Angeles. In the anthropological tradition, her name was changed to protect her identity.

2. A survey of book titles published in the 1990s indicates the ubiquitous use of "race" and "biracial theorizing." This uncritical theorizing and obsession with "race" only obfuscates and reproduces what is merely an ideological notion with no analytical value. As we enter the twenty-first century, the concept of race continues (with few exceptions) to provide the discursive or analytical basis for much of the work in the social sciences and humanities. Examples of some recent titles include *Two Nations: Black and White, Separate, Hostile, and Unequal* (Hacker 1992); *Chain Reaction: The Impact of Race, Rights, and Taxes on American Politics* (Edsall and Edsall 1991); *Race in America: The Struggle for Equality* (Hill and Jones 1993); *Race Matters* (West 1993); *Faded Dreams: The Politics and Economics of Race in America* (Carnoy 1994); *Facing Up to the American Dream: Race, Class, and the Soul of the Nation* (Hochchild 1995); *Turning Back: The Retreat from Racial Justice in American Thought and Policy* (Steinberg 1995); and *Faces at the Bottom of the Well* (Bell 1992). Several of these books present a glib "multicultural" narrative and fail to provide an analytical apparatus that moves beyond the black-white framework. For an excellent volume on the need for social policies that go beyond the binary black-white paradigm, see *Transforming Race Relations: A Public Policy Report* (Ong 2000).

3. The following paragraphs rely heavily on *Latino Metropolis* (Valle and Torres 2000).

4. There is an extensive literature critiquing the notion of "race" as a biological subdivision of the human population and a growing body of scientific evidence that undermines the nineteenth-century idea of "races" as natural, discrete, and fixed subdivisions of the human species, each with its distinct and variable cultural characteristics and capacity for "civilization" (Benedict 1983; Cavalli-Sforza and Cavalli-Sforza 1995; Miles 1989; Montagu 1974). In 1997, the American Anthropological Association drafted a statement on "race":

> The species is not divided into exclusive, genetically distinct, homogeneous groupings similar to subspecies, as the concept of "race" implies. All human groups share many features with other groups, and it is impossible to draw rigid boundaries around them. Genetically there are greater differences between individuals within a group defined popularly as a race than

there are between two "races." There are no pure "races," and no groups are physically, intellectually or morally superior, or inferior, to others. (1)

5. This point was made during a discussion about the role of the Asian American studies scholar at the seminar, "Chinese Diaspora in Southern California: Culture, Ethnicity, Community, and Asian American Studies," at California State University, Los Angeles, July 13, 1996.

6. Recent Asian immigrants tend to concentrate in new and old Chinatowns, Koreatown, Little Saigon, Little Phnom Penh, Little India, Manilatown, and the burgeoning multiethnic San Gabriel Valley, while Latinos are in the Pico-Union district, East Los Angeles, and the Anaheim-Santa Ana-Long Beach corridor.

7. In describing the population enumeration project—the "racializing" project—of the U.S. Census Bureau, Goldberg (1995) asserts that

from the project's inception, the Republic required enumeration of racial groups, formalized by constitutional mandate via census counts. . . . In the absence of explicit definitions of the racial categories, the census relied in its first half century on establishing the racial-body count upon the "commonsense" judgments of its all-white enumerators. Persons were racially named, the body politic measured, and resources distributed on the basis of the prevailing racial presumptions and mandated fractional assessments. The society was literally marked, and marked only, in broad strokes of black and white. (239)

It was in 1850 that distinctions began to appear for those considered "nonwhite," indicating "an emerging social commitment to gradations in color consciousness. The growing complexity of these social distinctions seemed to demand that enumerators be issued instruction schedules concerning the racial categories" (ibid., 239–40). The schedule of instructions for the 1890 count reflected not only the rapid diversification of the U.S. population but also the "intensifying administrative concern in the face of this expanding diversity with racial distinction, hierarchy, imposed division, and the symbolic and material challenges of miscegenational mixing" (ibid., 240).

8. The concept of racialization has been employed by U.S. scholars, among them Howard Winant. Winant (1994) uses the concept of "racialization" to "signify the extension of racial meaning to a previously racially unclassified relationship, social practice or group" (59). While there is much to admire and to learn from their theoretical and conceptual innovations, the authors' concept of racialization is grounded in "race relations" sociology—a sociology that reifies the notion of "race." This reification of "race" implies that racialized groups constitute a monolithic social category. In suggesting that "race" is an active subject—"an unstable and 'decentered' complex of social meanings"—the authors advance the notion that the idea of "race" is socially constructed. Yet they implicitly embrace and anchor their analysis of social movements and "racial formation" on an illusionary concept of "race." Furthermore, Omi and Winant

assign analytical status to the idea of "race" by claiming that "the concept of racial formation should treat race in the United States as a fundamental organizing principle of social relationship" (1986, 66). Their conceptualization of "race" in terms of shifting sets of meanings fails to capture racist expressions and exclusion, much of which is tied up with capital and labor formation. We maintain that racialization is grounded in class and production relations and the idea of "race" need not be explicitly used for a process of racialization to occur.

9. "Racial" polarization was the leading reason mentioned by respondents who indicated that the city had changed for the worst.

10. We follow the definition of Glick Schiller, Basch, and Blanc (1994) on "transmigrants": "transmigrants are immigrants whose daily lives depend on multiple and constant interconnections across international borders and whose public identities are configured in relationship to more than one nation-state" (48). In discussing the two adjectives of "diaspora"—"diasporic" and "diasporan"—Tololyan (1995), writing as the editor of *Diaspora*, notes that "diasporic" is "constructed on the model of and in rhyme with the term for another subnational collectivity, 'ethnic.' 'Diasporan,' presumably, is modeled on larger national and even continental terms, such as 'European,' 'African,' and 'American.'" In this chapter, we prefer the adjective "diasporic," as it describes migrants from the diaspora who have become "ethnic" in a larger national formation.

11. Robert Miles, lecture given at the Claremont Graduate School, Claremont, California, 1994.

NOTES TO CHAPTER 3

1. In 1974 the U.S. Supreme Court unanimously ruled that unlawful discrimination had taken place when Chinese-speaking students in San Francisco were taught in a language they could not understand. The *Lau v. Nichols* decision, while limited in scope, became the legal precedent in support of bilingual education programs across the country and remains the major legal precedent on language rights in the United States (Crawford 2000).

2. For the purpose of this discussion, the notion of linguistic rights is being used as defined by Tove Skutnabb-Kangas (2000)—that is, 1. the right to learn, use, be educated, and identify with one's mother tongue; 2. the right to learn the official language for the country in residence; 3. the right not to have a change of one's mother tongue imposed; and 4. the right to profit from the state education system, no matter what first language one learns.

3. Not all scholars ascribe significance to a nation-state thesis. For a competing perspective, see *Empire* by Michael Hardt and Antonio Negri (2000), where the authors posit that the nation-state has become fiction.

4. Neoliberal corporate interests seek to expand NAFTA rules to the entire

Western hemisphere by 2005. The Free Trade Area of the Americas (FTAA) in-cludes provisions that would increase the pressure to deregulate public services such as providing education, health care, and safe drinking water. It would im-pact thirty-four countries, affecting an estimated 800 million people. Labor movements and nongovernmental organizations (NGOs) across the hemisphere, along with a network of coalitions in the United States such as Jobs with Justice, are poised to oppose the passage of the FTAA.

5. We are cautious in our use of the notion of transcitizenship if it implies the occupation of a "third space" outside the U.S. political economy. We maintain that Mexican immigrants are part of the U.S. working class and not some imagi-nary "transnational community" apart from the U.S. nation-state. Gilbert Gon-zalez and Raul Fernandez (2003) argue that "what appears as 'third spaces' are in fact immigrant communities integrated into the nation-state and, for the most part, internal sources of cheap labor" (183).

6. On September 11, 2001, the twin towers of the World Trade Center in New York City were destroyed when two passenger airliners were hijacked and diverted to crash into each of the towers. The September 11 attacks generated xenophobic and anti-immigrant violence in some communities. The racialized discourse of the "Other" became especially prominent following the attacks, but it has also become problematic in the face of three decades of remarkably high rates of immigration into the United States. A symbolic politics encouraging fear and loathing of the "Other" is integral to crime and violence in American cities, but it was not until September 11 that urban violence became narrowly concep-tualized in terms of local issues of crime and crime control, independent of larger societal changes. On December 17, 2003, civil rights and immigrant defense or-ganizations filed a suit in federal court in New York challenging a post–Septem-ber 11 initiative by Attorney General John Ashcroft and the U.S. Department of Justice to enlist state and local police in the routine enforcement of federal immi-gration laws and charging that co-opting state and local police to make immigra-tion arrests undermines public safety and encourages racial profiling (National Council of La Raza 2003).

7. See Donaldo Macedo, Bessie Dendrinos, and Panayota Gounari's (2003) *The Hegemony of English* for an incisive discussion of the politics of English-only efforts in this country and abroad.

8. In "The Social Significance of English in Malawi," published in *World Englishes* 20(2) (July 2001), Alfred J. Matiki examines how the language policy in Malawi has entrenched the hegemony of English over Chichewa and other in-digenous languages, especially in the official domains of national life. Although both English and Chichewa are official languages, the language policy has cre-ated an asymmetrical relationship between the two by favoring English over Chichewa. Matiki explores the current role of English vis-à-vis Chichewa, based on its functions, range, and depth. His work further shows that the exclusive use

of English in the legislature, the judiciary, and mass media, among other domains, alienates the majority of Malawians who have no facility in this language and consequently limits their political rights in many respects. It is important, therefore, to institute a language plan that can more effectively guide the country in sustaining democracy, promoting the vitality, versatility, and stability of indigenous languages, and the preserving the rights of their speakers to participate in the national community.

NOTE TO CHAPTER 4

1. The Stanford 9 test has now been replaced with the California Assessment Test (CAT 6).

NOTES TO CHAPTER 5

1. For scholarly works that focus on "critical theories of race," see Richard Delgado, *Critical Race Theory: The Cutting Edge* (1995); Kimberlé Crenshaw, Neil Gotanda, Gary Peller, and Kendal Thomas, eds., *Critical Race Theory: The Key Writings That Formed the Movement* (1995); Mari Matsuda, Charles Lawrence, Richard Delgado, and Kimberlé Crenshaw, *Words That Wound: Critical Race Theory, Assaultive Speech, and the First Amendment* (1993); and Adrien Katherine Wing, ed., *Critical Race Feminism: A Reader* (1997); as well as writings by Michael Omi and Howard Winant, including *Racial Conditions* (Winant 1994).

2. Recent efforts to bring "class" into the debate are a positive conceptual and theoretical development. But we caution our colleagues not to fall into the trap of just adding "class" to the equation of other identities. As we argue in this volume, there is a need to sort out the salient theoretical underpinnings of an approach to class-based analysis that recognizes struggle and conflict as a means of social change. In these chapters, we attempt to specify the meaning of a Marxist-informed class-based approach that views class and classes in a capitalist society in terms of their structural position within production relations. The Marxist theory of modes of production is central and necessary to this project of deracialization in capitalist society.

3. Also see the article by Elizabeth M. Iglesias (1998), "Out of the Shadow: Marking Intersections in and between Asian Pacific American Critical Legal Scholarship and Latina/o Critical Theory," where she issues a call "for LatCrit theory to move beyond abstract race/class debates by centering political economy and the production of class hierarchies" (95).

4. Care must be taken not to speak of the state and capital in monolithic terms, as they are sometimes at odds. See Ralph Miliband's (1989) *Divided Societies: Class Struggle in Contemporary Capitalism* and Nicos Poulantzas's (1973)

Political Power and Social Classes for competing normative views of the state in capitalist societies, though both would agree on the heterogeneity of capital and the state.

5. C. L. R. James addresses the "Negro Question" in *The Historical Development of the Negroes in American Society* (1943), which was "originally circulated within the Worker's Party as a memorandum dated 20 December 1943. It was submitted to the 1944 National Convention of the Worker's party, and first published as 'Negroes and the Revolution: Resolution of the Minority' in The New International, January 1945" (McLemee 1996, 149). Although James identifies the "dangers" of the "chauvinism of the oppressed" in this essay, he makes a case that "the only way to overcome them is to recognize its fundamental progressive tendency and to distinguish sharply between the chauvinisms of the oppressed and the chauvinism of the oppressor" (McLemee 1996, 86). However, more than sixty years later, what we have learned from a myriad of antiracism struggles rooted in nationalism and identity politics is that chauvinism of any persuasion ultimately confines, restricts, and delimits the political solidarity required to challenge the totalizing impact of capitalism in this country and around the world.

6. One of the most significant theoretical contributions made during the post–civil rights era regarding questions of racialized identities was formulated by radical feminists of color who presented the most sophisticated articulations of the intersectionality argument, with its often cited mantra of "race, class, and gender."

7. More than fifty years after the publication of *Caste, Class, and Race* by Doubleday in 1948, many scholars continue to attribute Marxist analytical status to the work of Oliver Cox. We argue that this is misleading because Cox, who retained "race" as the central category of analysis in his work, remained staunchly anchored in a "race relations" paradigm.

NOTES TO CHAPTER 6

An earlier version of this chapter appeared as an article in *Latino Studies* 1(2) (2003).

1. We underscore here Silvio Torres-Saillant's (2003) warning that we "risk mistaking increased visibility [of Latinos and Latinas] in the media and the entertainment industry for community empowerment" (27) or for scholarly integration of Latino scholarship into the arena of public debate.

2. For some excellent examples of comparative work on Latinos and Latinas, see Juan Poblete, ed., *Critical Latin American and Latino Studies* (2003), which includes articles by scholars such as George Yudice, Tómas Almaguer, Angie Chabran-Dernersesian, Juan Flores, and Francés Aparicio; Juanita Díaz-Cotto, *Gender, Ethnicity, and the State: Latina and Latino Prison Politics* (1996); Mary

Pardo, *Mexican American Women Activists: Identity and Resistance in Two Los Angeles Communities* (1998); Frank Bonilla, Edwin Melendez, and Maria de los Angeles Torres, eds., *Borderless Borders: U.S. Latinos, Latin Americans, and the Paradox of Interdependence* (1998); and the collection of writings on Latinos *Latino/a Thought: Culture, Politics, and Society,* edited by Francisco H. Vázquez and Rodolfo D. Torres (2003).

3. For excellent contributions to the growing field of Chicana, gender, and cultural studies, see Rosa Linda Fregosa, *MeXicana Encounters: The Making of Social Identities on the Borderlands* (2003); and Gabriela F. Arredondo, Aída Hurtado, Norma Klahn, Olga Nájera-Ramirez, and Patricia Zavalla, eds., *Chicana Feminisms: A Critical Reader* (2003).

4. The racialization of Latino men bites most obviously at the level of class and the schooling experience. Although Latino men in the United States range in employment from street hustlers to day laborers through to corporate lawyers and medical doctors and so on, numerically they are most often found in the service sector and in traditional blue-collar occupations. Currently, Latinos account for 12.5 percent of the nation's population, or more than 35 million persons (U.S. Census Bureau 2001a, 1), yet only a little more than 2 million Latino males (compared with more than 33 million "non-Hispanic white males") hold managerial or professional positions in the workplace, out of a total of more than 43 million such positions currently occupied in the United States (U.S. Census Bureau 2001b, 1). In addition, many Latino men are members of the "working poor," working long hours at two or more jobs, but still are not able to make ends meet (Valle and Torres 2000). In addition, the majority of Latino men are not university graduates. By 2000, for example, only a little more than 2.3 million "Hispanic" males held a bachelor's degree or higher, compared with 19.3 million "non-Hispanic white" males (U.S. Census Bureau 2001c, 1). This contrasts dramatically with Latino males' incarceration rates; by mid-2000 Latino males in their twenties and thirties accounted for 15.1 percent of prison inmates in the United States, and 4 percent of all Latino males, or 280 per 100,000 Latino residents, are currently in prison (for a total of 207,985 men), compared with 132 per 100,000 "non-Hispanic white" males, or 1.7 percent of the total white male population (Beck and Karberg 2001, 1, 7). In a "postindustrial" economy geared toward symbolic and analytic work, a university degree becomes a bottom-line criterion for economic opportunity and mobility. Education inequities experienced by Latino males, however, begin long before university. A growing area of education research is the "problem" of boys and their literacy performance at school. While this issue is in itself a problematic cultural construction (Rowan et al. 2002), there remains a concern that the increasing "feminization" of education, in terms of the number of female teachers compared with male, is encouraging many boys to "act out" masculinities that value literacy failure, sexism, and trouble-making (Martino and Meyenn 2001; Skelton

2001). While boys, masculinities, and literacy education garner widespread interest and needful attention, the consistently low performance of Latino boys in school literacy tests and subjects continues to be shuffled under the carpet of skills-based remediation classes and remains underresearched and unaddressed in education.

Young Latino men have consistently dropped out of high school in large numbers over the past thirty years. The current dropout rate for Latino boys as a group is not readily available, but in general, significantly more boys than girls drop out of high school (NCES 2001). In 2000, Latinos accounted disproportionately for 27.8 percent of all dropouts in the United States aged sixteen to twenty-four years, compared with 13.1 percent of the African American student population, 3.8 percent of the Asian/Pacific Islander student population, and 6.9 percent for "non-Hispanic white" students for the same period (NCES 2001, 5). Most important, socioeconomic structural factors shape Latino men and their masculinities. Being in the United States greatly affects these men because they learn new traditions of fatherhood, brotherhood, fraternalism, and camaraderie, but they also learn new means of sex, gender, and sexual orientation discrimination. It still remains to be seen what, if anything, other U.S. men have learned from Latino men. Our volatile and reactionary U.S. sex-gender system remains a key social force in shaping men's identities. A fundamental systemic and ideological shift will be necessary to improve the material conditions for Latino men. Social, economic, and political transformations through the creation of better paying jobs and improvement of the educational system will enhance prospects for Latino men, their families and just as importantly, for Latina women as well.

5. For examples of work focused on critical race theory, see Richard Delgado, *Critical Race Theory: The Cutting Edge* (1995); Kimberlé Crenshaw, Neil Gotanda, Gary Peller, and Kendal Thomas, eds., *Critical Race Theory: The Key Writings That Formed the Movement* (1995); Adrien Katherine Wing, ed., *Critical Race Feminism: A Reader* (1997; 2d ed., 2003); and Lani Guinier and Gerald Torres, *The Miner's Canary: Enlisting Race, Resisting Power, Transforming Democracy* (2002).

6. For a variety of perspectives on Latinidad, see Frances Aparicio and Susana Chavez-Silverman, eds., *Tropicalizations: Transcultural Representations of Latinidad* (1997); Juana María Rodríguez, *Queer Latinidad: Identity, Practices, Discursive Spaces* (2003); Chon Noriega, "El Hilo Latino: Representation, Identity, and National Culture" (1993); David Román and Alberto Sandoval, "Caught in the Web: Latinidad, AIDS, and Allegory in *Kiss of the Spider Woman*, the Musical" (1995); and the forthcoming special issue on Latinidades in *Latino Studies* (2004) to be edited by Ralph Cintro and Frances Aparicio.

7. For an excellent review of contemporary debates on globalization, see David Held and Anthony McGrew, *Globalization/Anti-Globalization* (2002).

8. In the last decade, *Monthly Review* has published some of the most inci-

sive critiques and formidable interrogations into the globalization debate. These authors included Ellen Meiksins Wood, Harry Magdoff, Frances Fox Piven, Robert McChesney, Peter Meiksins, Bill Tabb, and Istvan Meszaros.

9. For some recent examples of Latino scholarship that engage questions of Latino immigration and/or citizenship with respect to wider cultural and social issues of racialized identities, see Nicholas De Genova and Ana Ramos-Zaya, *Latino Crossings: Mexicans, Puerto Ricans, and the Politics of Race and Citizenship* (2003); Hector R. Cordero-Guzman, Robert C. Smith, and Ramon Grosfoguel, *Migration, Transnationalization, and Race in a Changing New York* (2001); Michael Jones-Correa, *Between Two Nations: The Political Predicament of Latinos in New York City* (1998); Roberto Suro, *Strangers among Us* (1999); David R. Maciel and María Herrera-Sobek, *Culture across Borders: Mexican Immigration and Popular Culture* (1998); Silvio Torres-Saillant and Ramona Hernandez, *The Dominican Americans* (1998); and William Flores and Rina Benmayor, *Latino Cultural Citizenship: Claiming Identity, Space, and Rights* (1997).

10. For a study that might serve as a guide for future work on Latino citizenship studies, see the theoretically rich and original work on Cambodian Americans and their integration into the U.S. political economy by Aihwa Ong in *Buddha Is Hiding: Refugees, Citizenship, and the New America* (2003).

11. Progressive Puerto Rican scholars did not embrace the "internal colony" model to the same extent as their Chicano counterparts. In 1972 a seminar was held at Stanford University where Chicano, Puerto Rican, African American, and Latin American scholars attempted to forge a common reference for inequality, while examining questions of imperialism and dependency theory, along with discussion and critique of the internal colonial model. The seminar included such scholars as Frank Bonilla, Ronald Bailey, Evelina Dagnino, Guillermo Flores, Robert Girling, and Fernando Henrique Cardoso (Bonilla and Girling 1973). Also see Frank Bonilla, *Labor Migration under Capitalism: The Puerto Rican Experience* (History Task Force 1979) and other fine works by Puerto Rican scholars published by the *Centro de Estudios Puertorriqueños* at Hunter College over the last fifteen years. For those interested in an excellent Marxist interpretation of Puerto Rican history, see Manuel Maldonado-Denis, *Puerto Rico: A Socio-Historic Interpretation* (1972).

12. For an example of the application of the internal colony model in Chicano studies, see Mario Barrera, Carlos Munoz, and Charles Ornelas, "The Barrio as an Internal Colony" (1972). For a critique of the model from writers representing two different strands of Marxist theory, see Gilbert Gonzalez, "A Critique of the Internal Colonial Model" (1974); and Tomás Almaguer, "Ideological Distortions in Recent Chicano Historiography: The Internal Model and Chicano Historical Interpretation" (1987).

13. For a variety of perspectives on social movements, politics, and Latinos

in the United States, see Ignacio M. García, *Chicanismo: The Forging of a Militant Ethos among Mexican Americans* (1997); Rodolfo F. Acuña, *Anything but Mexican: Chicanos in Contemporary Los Angeles* (1991); Jose E. Cruz, *Identity and Power: Puerto Rican Politics and the Challenge of Ethnicity* (1998); Andrés Torres and José E. Velázquez, *The Puerto Rican Movement: Voices from the Diaspora* (1998); Rodolfo D. Torres and George Katsiaficas, *Latino Social Movements* (1999); and Victor Valle and Rodolfo D. Torres, *Latino Metropolis* (2000).

14. See *Monthly Review*'s issue "The New Economy: Myth and Reality," 52(11) (April 2001), for an incisive discussion about the impact of the internalization of capital on the plight of workers, the labor movement, the media, and world markets.

15. See Doug Henwood, *After the New Economy* (2003); and William Baumol, Alan Blinder, and Edward Wolff, *Downsizing in America: Reality, Causes, and Consequences* (2003).

16. For a thoughtful Latin American studies perspective on the history of racism, see the following publications by Marisol de la Cadena: *Indigenous Mestizos: The Politics of Race and Culture in Cuzco, Peru, 1919–1991* (2000) and "The Racial Politics of Culture and Silent Racism in Peru" (2001). For a different perspective, see the work of Peruvian sociologist and world-systems theorist Anibal Quijano (2000) who argues that the modern history of racism actually begins with European classifications of native peoples in the sixteenth century. Quijano's development of the notion of "coloniality of power" to describe diverse racial/ethnic hierarchies in the context of a capitalist world system is ambitious and interesting, but not entirely convincing. With this postdependency paradigm, Quijano attempts to provide an alternative to the traditional dichotomy between cultural studies and political economy.

17. The groundbreaking work of Robert Miles has strongly influenced our views on the question of "race." See *Racism and Migrant Labor* (1982); *Racism* (1989); *Racism after "Race Relations"* (1993); and *Racism* (2d ed., co-authored with Malcolm Brown, 2003). As we noted in the introduction, Paul Gilroy, an early critic of Miles, recently has advanced a similar position in his book *Against Race: Imagining Political Culture beyond the Colorline* (2000).

18. For an excellent study on community-building strategies for building democratic institutions, see Thad Williamson, David Imbroscio, and Gar Alperovitz, *Making a Place for Community: Local Democracy in a Global Era* (2002). For a discussion of an alternative political global program to neoliberalism, see Hilary Wainwright, *Reclaim the State: Experiments in Popular Democracy* (2003).

19. See Bob Jessop, *The Future of the Capitalist State* (2003).

20. During the 1990s, the initiative process (once envisioned as a democratizing, legislative vehicle for the masses) became co-opted as an effective tool for

neoliberal interests in California. Several conservative initiatives were success-fully passed by voters including Proposition 227, which called for the elimina-tion of bilingual education in public schools; Proposition 187, which called for the elimination of health, education, and welfare benefits to undocumented im-migrants; and Proposition 209, which called for the elimination of race as a de-terminant in educational admission to state colleges and universities. In a similar fashion, neoconservative interests in California utilized the recall process in 2003, heavily financing the campaign to oust Democratic Governor Gray Davis and elect Republican newcomer and actor Arnold Schwarzenegger—of *Termina-tor* fame—to the governorship.

Bibliography

Acuña, Rodolfo F. 1996. *Anything but Mexican: Chicanos in Contemporary Los Angeles.* New York and London: Verso.

Allen, James P., and Eugene Turner. 1997. *The Ethnic Quilt: Population Diversity in Southern California.* Northridge, Calif.: Center for Geographical Studies, California State University.

Almaguer, Tomás. 1987. "Ideological Distortions in Recent Chicano Historiography: The Internal Model and Chicano Historical Interpretation." *Aztlán* 18(1) (Spring).

Amariglio, Jack L., Stephen A. Resnick, and Richard D. Wolff. 1988. "Class, Power, and Culture." In Cary Nelson and Lawrence Grossberg, eds., *Marxism and the Interpretation of Culture.* Urbana and Chicago: University of Illinois Press.

Amaro, H., R. Vega, and D. Valencia. 2001. "Gender, Context, and HIV Prevention among Latinos." In Marilyn Aguirre-Molina, Carlos W. Molina, and Ruth Enid Zambrana, eds., *Health Issues in the Latino Community.* San Francisco: Jossey Bass.

American Anthropological Association. 1997. "Is It 'Race'? Anthropology on Human Diversity." *Anthropology Newsletter* 38(4) (April): 1, 5.

Amit-Talai, Vered, and Caroline Knowles, eds. 1996. *Re-Situating Identities: The Politics of Race, Ethnicity, and Culture.* Peterborough, Ont.: Broadview Press.

Anderson, Benedict. 1991. *Imagined Communities.* London: Verso.

Anner, John. 1996. *Beyond Identity Politics.* Boston: South End Press.

Anthias, Floya, and Nica Yuval-Davis, in association with Harriet Cain. 1992. *Racialized Boundaries: Race, Nation, Gender, and Color and the Anti-Racist Struggle.* London: Routledge.

Aparicio, Frances R., and Susana Chavez-Silverman, eds. 1997. *Tropicalizations: Transcultural Representations of Latinidad.* Dartmouth, N.H.: Dartmouth College/University Press of New England.

Appiah, K. Anthony. 1995. "The Uncompleted Argument: Du Bois and the Illusion of Race." In Linda Bell and David Blumenfeld, eds., *Overcoming Racism and Sexism.* Lanham, Md.: Rowman and Littlefield.

———. 1996. "Race, Culture, Identity: Misunderstood Connections." In K. Anthony Appiah and Amy Gutmann, eds., *Color Conscious: The Political Morality of Race*. Princeton, N.J.: Princeton University Press.

Apple, Michael. 1995. *Education and Power* (2d ed.). New York: Routledge.

Arredondo, Gabriela F., Aída Hurtado, Norma Klahn, Olga Nájera-Ramirez, and Patricia Zavalla. 2003. *Chicana Feminisms: A Critical Reader*. Durham, N.C.: Duke University Press.

Azevedo, K., and H. Ochoa Bogue. 2001. "Health and Occupational Risks of Latinos Living in Rural America." In Marilyn Aguirre-Molina, Carlos W. Molina, and Ruth Enid Zambrana, eds., *Health Issues in the Latino Community*. San Francisco: Jossey Bass.

Baldwin, James. 1988. "A Talk to Teachers." In Rick Simonson and Scott Walker, eds., *Multicultural Literacy*, 3–12. Saint Paul, Minn: Graywolf Press.

———. 1998. "On Being 'White' . . . and Other Lies." In David Roediger, ed., *Black on White*. New York: Schocken Books.

Balibar, Etienne. 1991. "Es Gibt Keinen Staat in Europe: Racism and Politics in Europe." In *New Left Review* 185: 5–19.

———. 2003. "Election/Selection." Keynote delivered at Traces: Race, Deconstruction and Critical Theory Conference. University of California, Irvine (April 10): 1–19.

Balibar, Etienne, and Immanuel Wallerstein. 1991. *Race, Nation, Class: Ambiguous Identities*. London: Verso.

Ball, Wendy, and John Solomos. 1990. *Race and Local Politics*. New York: Macmillan.

Banton, Michael. 1967. *Race Relations*. London: Tavistock.

———. 1987. *Racial Theories*. Cambridge: Cambridge University Press.

Barkan, Elazar. 1992. *The Retreat of Scientific Racism: Changing Concepts of Race in Britain and the United States between the World Wars*. Cambridge: Cambridge University Press.

Barnes, Robin. 1990. "Race Consciousness: The Thematic Content of Racial Distinctiveness in Critical Race Scholarship." *Harvard Law Review* 103: 1864–71.

Barnet, Richard J., and John Cavanagh. 1994. *Global Dreams: Imperial Corporations and the New World Order*. New York: Touchstone Books.

Barot, Rohit, and John Bird. 2001. "Racialization: The Genealogy and Critique of a Concept." *Ethnic and Racial Studies* 24(4) (4 July): 601–18.

Barrera, Mario. 1979. *Race and Class in the Southwest*. Notre Dame, Ind.: University of Notre Dame Press.

———. 1984. "Chicano Class Structure." In Eugene E. Garcia, Francisco A. Lomeli, and Isidro D. Ortiz, eds., *Chicano Studies: A Multidisciplinary Approach*, 40–55. New York: Teachers College Press.

Barrera, Mario, Carlos Muñoz, and Charles Ornelas. 1972. "The Barrio as an Internal Colony." *Urban Affairs Annual Review* 6: 465–98.

Baumol, William J., Alan S. Blinder, and Edward N. Wolff. 2003. *Downsizing in America: Reality, Causes, and Consequences.* New York: Russell Sage Foundation.

Beck, Allen J., and Jennifer C. Karberg. 2001. "Prison and Jail Inmates at Midyear 2000." *Bureau of Justice Statistics Bulletin* (March). Washington, D.C.: U.S. Department of Justice.

Bell, Derrick. 1992. *Faces at the Bottom of the Well.* New York: Basic Books.

Bellah, Robert N., Richard Madsen, William M. Sullivan, Nann Swidler, and Steven M. Tipton. 1985. *Habits of the Heart: Individualism and Commitment in American Life.* New York: Harper and Row.

Belsie, L. 2002. "Labor More Militant as Economy Teeters." Boston: *Christian Science Monitor* (22 August).

Benedict, Ruth. 1983. *Race and Racism.* London: Routledge and Kegan Paul.

Blauner, Robert. 1992. "Talking Past Each Other: Black and White Languages of Race." *American Prospect* 10: 55–64.

Bonilla, Frank, and Robert Girling. 1973. *Structures of Dependency.* A monograph of papers presented at a conference at Stanford University.

Bonilla, Frank, Edwin Melendez, and Maria de Los Angeles Torres. 1998. *Borderless Border: U.S. Latinos, Latin Americans, and the Paradox of Interdependence.* Philadelphia: Temple University Press.

Borthwick, Mark. 1992. *Pacific Century: The Emergence of Modern Pacific Asia.* Boulder, Colo.: Westview Press.

Bowles, Samuel, and Herbert Gintis. 1976. *Schooling in Capitalist America.* New York: Basic Books.

Cantu, Lionel. 2000. "Entre Hombres/Between Men: Latino Masculinities and Homosexualities." In Peter Nard, ed., *Gay Masculinities.* Thousand Oaks, Calif.: Sage.

Caputo-Pearl, Alex. 2001. "Challenging High-Stakes Standardized Testing: Working to Build an Anti-Racist Progressive Social Movement in Public Education." Working Paper for Coalition for Educational Justice, Los Angeles, California.

Carnoy, Martin. 1994. *Faded Dreams: The Politics and Economics of Race in America.* Cambridge: Cambridge University Press.

Castles, Stephen. 1996. "The Racisms of Globalization." In Ellie Vasta and Stephen Castle, eds., *The Teeth Are Smiling: The Persistence of Racism in Australia,* 17–45. St. Leonards, New South Wales: Allen and Unwin.

Cavalli-Sforza, Luigi Luca, and Francesco Cavalli-Sforza. 1995. *The Great Human Diasporas: The History of Diversity and Evolution.* Reading, Mass.: Helix Books.

Chan, Sucheng, ed. 1991. *Entry Denied: Exclusion and the Chinese Community in America, 1882–1943*. Philadelphia: Temple University Press.

Check, Joseph. 2002. *Politics, Language, and Culture: A Critical Look at Urban School Reform*. Westport, Conn.: Praeger.

Cordero-Guzman, Hector R., Robert C. Smith, and Ramon Grosfoguel. 2001. *Migration, Transnationalization, and Race in a Changing New York*. Philadelphia: Temple University Press.

Cox, Oliver. 1970. *Caste, Class, and Race: A Study in Social Dynamics*. New York: Monthly Review Press.

Crawford, James. 2000. *At War with Diversity: U.S. Language Policy in an Age of Anxiety*. Clevedon, U.K.: Multilingual Matters.

Crenshaw, Kimberlé, Neil Gotanda, Gary Peller, and Kendal Thomas, eds. 1995. *Critical Race Theory: The Key Writings That Formed the Movement*. New York: New Press.

Crouch, Gregory. 1992. "O.C. Businesses Learn Hard Lesson in Mexico." *Los Angeles Times* (Orange County edition) (16 August): A1, A28, A30.

Cruz, Jon. 1996. "From Farce to Tragedy: Reflections in the Reification of Race at Century's End." In Avery F. Gordon and Christopher Newfield, eds., *Mapping Multiculturalism*. Minneapolis: University of Minnesota Press.

Cruz, Jose E. 1998. *Identity and Power: Puerto Rican Politics and the Challenge of Ethnicity*. Philadelphia: Temple University Press.

"CSAP 2002: A Guide to Results of the Student Assessment Tests." 2002. *Rocky Mountain News*, Denver, Colorado (1 August).

Cuban, Larry. 2001. *Oversold and Underused: Computers in the Classroom*. Cambridge, Mass.: Harvard University Press.

Darder, Antonia. 1991. *Culture and Power in the Classroom*. Westport, Conn.: Bergin and Garvey.

———. 2002. *Reinventing Paulo Freire*. Boulder, Colo.: Westview Press.

Darder, Antonia, and Rodolfo D. Torres. 1997. *The Latino Studies Reader: Culture, Economy, and Society*. Oxford: Blackwell.

———. 1999. "Shattering the Race Lens: Toward a Critical Theory of Racism." In Robert Tai and Mary Kenyatta, eds., *Critical Ethnicity*. Lanham, Md.: Rowman and Littlefield.

———. 2002. "Mapping Latino Studies: Critical Reflections on Class and Theory." *Latino Studies* 1(2).

Davis, Angela. 1996. "Gender, Class, and Multiculturalism." In Avery F. Gordon and Christopher Newfield, eds., *Mapping Multiculturalisms*. Minneapolis: University of Minnesota Press.

Davis, Mike. 1990. *City of Quartz*. London: Verso.

———. 2001. *Magical Urbanism: Latinos Reinvent the U.S. City*. New York: Verso.

De Genova, Nicholas, and Ana Y. Ramos-Zayas. 2003. *Latino Crossings: Mexicans, Puerto Ricans, and the Politics of Race and Citizenship.* New York and London: Routledge.

de la Cadena, Marisol. 2000. *Indigenous Mestizos: The Politics of Race and Culture in Cuzco, Peru, 1919–1991.* Durham, N.C.: Duke University Press.

———. 2001. "The Racial Politics of Culture and Silent Racism in Peru." Project report for the United Nations Research Institute for Social Development (UNRISD), Geneva, Switzerland. (Accessed on-line at http://www.unrisd/ website/projects.nsf/)

De León, Arnoldo. 1983. *They Called Them Greasers: Anglo Attitudes toward Mexicans in Texas, 1821–1900.* Austin: University of Texas Press.

Delgado, Richard. 1995. *Critical Race Theory: The Cutting Edge.* Philadelphia: Temple University Press.

Delgado, Richard, and Jean Stefancic. 2001. *Critical Race Theory.* New York: New York University Press.

Delgado Bernal, Dolores. 2002. "Critical Race Theory, Latino Critical Theory, and Critical Raced-Gendered Epistemologies: Recognizing Students of Color as Holders and Creators of Knowledge." *Qualitative Inquiry* 8(1): 105–26.

Delgado-Moreira, Juan. 1997. "Cultural Citizenship and the Creation of European Identity." *Electronic Journal of Sociology* (ISSN 1198) 3655: 1–19.

"Demographic and Health Snapshot of the U.S. Hispanic/Latino Population 2002." Atlanta: Centers for Disease Control and Prevention Department of Health and Human Services. (Accessed on-line at http://www.cdc.gov)

Díaz-Cotto, Juanita. 1996. *Gender, Ethnicity, and the State: Latina and Latino Prison Politics.* New York: New York University Press.

Du Bois, W. E. B. 1989/1903. *The Souls of Black Folk.* New York: Bantam Books.

Dunn, Robert. 1998. *Identity Crisis.* Minneapolis: University of Minnesota Press.

Eagleton, Terry. 2000. *The Idea of Culture.* Oxford: Blackwell.

Edsall, Thomas, and Mary Edsall. 1991. *Chain Reaction: The Impact of Race, Rights, and Taxes on American Politics.* New York: W. W. Norton.

Essed, Philomena. 1991. *Understanding Everyday Racism: An Interdisciplinary Theory.* Newbury Park: Sage.

Faryna, Stan, Brad Stetson, and Joseph Conti. 1997. *Black and Right: The Bold New Voice of Black Conservatives in America.* Westport, Conn.: Praeger.

Faux, Jeff. 2002. "Rethinking the Global Political Economy." Speech given at the Asia-Europe-U.S. Progressive Scholars' Forum: Globalization and Innovation of Politics, Japan (11–13 April).

Fears, Darryl. 2002. "People of Color Who Never Felt They Were Black: Racial

Labels Surprise Many Latino Immigrants." *Washington Post* (26 December): A1.

Fields, Barbara Jean. 1990. "Slavery, Race, and Ideology in the United States of America." *New Left Review* 181: 95–118.

———. 2001. "Whiteness, Racism, and Identity." In *International Labor and Working Class History* 60 (Fall): 48–56.

Figueroa, Richard, and Eugene Garcia. 1994. "Issues in Testing Students from Culturally and Linguistically Diverse Backgrounds." *Multicultural Education* 2(1) (Fall): 10–19.

Flores, William V. and Rina Benmayor. 1997. *Latino Cultural Citizenship: Claiming Identity, Space, and Rights.* Boston: Beacon Press.

Fredrickson, George M. 1981. *White Supremacy.* New York: Oxford University Press.

———. 1995. *Black Liberation: A Comparative History of Black Ideologies in the United States and South Africa.* New York: Oxford University Press.

———. 1996. "Far from the Promised Land." *New York Review of Books* 43(7) (18 April): 16–20.

———. 1997. *The Comparative Imagination: On the History of Racism, Nationalism, and Social Movements.* Berkeley: University of California Press.

———. 2002. *Racism: A Short History.* Princeton, N.J.: Princeton University Press.

Fregosa, Rosa Linda. 2003. *MeXicana Encounters: The Making of Social Identities on the Borderlands.* Berkeley: University of California Press.

Gann, Rose. 2000. "Postmodern Perspectives on Race and Racism: Help or Hindrance?" Paper presented at the Political Studies Association, UK, 50th Annual Conference, London (10–13 April).

———. 2003. "Race Politics and the Racial State." Paper presented at the Political Studies Association, UK, 53rd Annual Conference, Leicester, England (15–17 April).

García, Ignacio M. 1997. *Chicanismo: The Forging of a Militant Ethos among Mexican Americans.* Tucson: University of Arizona Press.

Gates, Henry Louis, Jr. 1997. *Thirteen Ways of Looking at a Black Man.* New York: Random House.

Gil, Andres, and William A. Vega. 2001. "Latino Drug Use: Scope, Risk Factors, and Reduction Strategies." In Marilyn Aguirre-Molina, Carlos W. Molina, and Ruth Enid Zambrana, eds., *Health Issues in the Latino Community.* San Francisco: Jossey Bass.

Gilroy, Paul. 1987. *"There Ain't No Black in the Union Jack": The Cultural Politics of Race and Nation.* London: Hutchinson.

———. 1991. *"There Ain't No Black in the Union Jack": The Cultural Politics of Race and Nation.* Chicago: University of Chicago Press.

———. 2000. *Against Race: Imagining Political Culture beyond the Colorline.* Cambridge, Mass: Harvard University Press.

———. 2002. *There Ain't No Black in the Union Jack.* London: Routledge.

Gimenez, Martha E. 1999. "Latino Politics—Class Struggle: Reflections on the Future of Latino Politics." In Rodolfo D. Torres and George Katsiaficas, eds., *Latino Social Movements: Historical and Theoretical Perspectives.* New York and London: Routledge.

Glick Schiller, Nina, Linda Basch, and Cristina Szanton Blanc. 1994. "From Immigrant to Transmigrant: Theorizing Transnational Migration." *Anthropological Quarterly* 68(1) (January): 48–63.

Goldberg, David Theo. 1990. *The Anatomy of Racism.* Minneapolis: University of Minnesota Press.

———. 1993. *Racist Culture: Philosophy and the Politics of Meaning.* Oxford: Blackwell.

———. 1995. "Made in the USA: Racial Mixing 'n' Matching." In Naomi Zack, ed., *American Mixed Race: The Culture of Microdiversity,* 237–55. Lanham, Md.: Rowman and Littlefield.

Gonzalez, Gilbert. 1974. "A Critique of the Internal Colonial Model." *Latin American Perspective* (Spring): 154–62.

Gonzalez, G. Gilbert, and Raul A. Fernandez. 2003. *A Century of Chicano History: Empire, Nations, and Migrations.* New York: Routledge.

Gonzalez, Juan. 2000. *A History of Latinos in America: Harvest of Empire.* New York: Viking.

Gorz, Andre. 1968. *Strategy for Labor.* Boston: Beacon Press.

Gramsci, Antonio. 1971. *Selections from Prison Notebook.* New York: International Publishers.

Graves, Joseph L., Jr. 2001. *The Emperor's New Clothes: Biological Theories of Race at the New Millennium.* New Brunswick, N.J.: Rutgers University Press.

Greider, William. 1997. *One World, Ready or Not: The Manic Logic of Global Capitalism.* New York: Simon and Schuster.

Grosfoguel, Ramon, and Chloe S. Georas. 1996. "The Racialization of Latino Caribbean Migrants in the New York Metropolitan Area." *Centro: Focus en Foco* 8(1–2): 193.

Guillaumin, Colette. 1972. *L'Ideologie Raciste.* Paris: Mouton.

———. 1980. "The Idea of Race and Its Elevation to Autonomous Scientific and Legal Status in UNESCO." In *Sociological Theories: Race and Colonialism.* Paris: UNESCO.

———. 1995. *Racism, Sexism, Power, and Ideology.* London: Routledge.

Guinier, Lani, and Gerald Torres. 2002. *The Miner's Canary: Enlisting Race, Resisting Power, Transforming Democracy.* Cambridge, Mass.: Harvard University Press.

Gutmann, M. C. 1996. "Meanings of Macho: The Cultural Politics of Masculinity in Mexico City." In Ray González, ed., *Muy Macho: Latino Men Confront Their Manhood*. New York: Anchor Books.

Guy-Sheftall, Beverly. 1995. *Words of Fire: An Anthology of African American Feminist Thought*. New York: New Press.

Hacker, Andrew. 1992. *Two Nations: Black and White, Separate, Hostile, and Unequal*. New York: Scribner.

Hall, Stuart. 1980. "Cultural Studies: Two Paradigms." *Media Culture and Society* 2: 57.

Hardt, Michael, and Antonio Negri. 2000. *Empire*. Cambridge, Mass.: Harvard University Press.

Harris, C. 1998. "Whiteness as Property." In David Roediger, ed., *Black on White: Black Writers on What It Means to Be White*. New York: Schocken Books.

Harvey, David. 1990. *The Condition of Postmodernity: An Enquiry into the Origins of Culture Change*. Oxford: Blackwell.

Hatcher, Richard, and Barry Troyna. 1993. "Racialization and Children." In Cameron McCarthy and Warren Crichlow, eds., *Race, Identity, and Representation in Education*, 109–25. New York: Routledge.

Held, David, and Anthony McGrew. 2002. *Globalization/Anti-Globalization*. Cambridge: Polity.

Henwood, Doug. 2003. *After the New Economy*. New York: New Press.

Herrnstein, Richard J., and Charles Murray. 1994. *The Bell Curve: Intelligence and Class Structure in American Life*. New York: Free Press.

Heubert, J., and R. Hauser. 1999. "High Stakes: Testing for Tracking, Promotion, and Graduation." Committee on Appropriate Test Use, Board on Testing and Assessment, Commission on Behavioral and Social Sciences and Education, and National Research Council. Washington D.C.: National Academy Press.

Hill, Herbert, and James E. Jones, eds. 1993. *Race in America: The Struggle for Equality*. Madison: University of Wisconsin Press.

History Task Force. 1979. *Labor Migration under Capitalism: The Puerto Rican Experience*. New York: Monthly Review Books.

Hochchild, Jennifer. 1995. *Facing Up to the American Dream: Race, Class, and the Soul of the Nation*. Princeton, N.J.: Princeton University Press.

hooks, bell. 1989. *Talking Back*. Boston: South End Press.

———. 1990. *Yearning: Race, Gender, and Cultural Politics*. Boston: South End Press.

———. 1995. *Killing Rage: Ending Racism*. New York: Henry Holt.

Hu-DeHart, Evelyn. 1994. "Latin America in Asia-Pacific Perspective." In Arif Dirlik, ed., *What Is in a Rim: Critical Perspectives on the Pacific Regional Idea*. Boulder, Colo.: Westview Press.

Hune, Shirley. 1995. "Rethinking Race: Paradigms and Policy Formation." *Amerasia Journal* 21(1–2): 29–40.

Iglesias, Elizabeth M. 1998. "Out of the Shadow: Marking Intersections in and between Asian Pacific American Critical Legal Scholarship and Latina/o Critical Theory." *Third World Law Review* 19: 349–83.

———. 1999. "Foreword: Democracy, Identity, Communicative Power, Inter/National Labor Rights, and the Evolution of LatCrit Theory and Community." *University of Miami Law Review* 53: 575–682.

Isaac, Jeffrey C. 1992. *Arendt, Camus, and Modern Rebellion.* New Haven, Conn.: Yale University Press.

Jessop, Bob. 1991. "Post-Fordism and the State." In Ash Amin, ed., *Post-Fordism: A Reader.* Oxford: Blackwell.

———. 2003. *The Future of the Capitalist State.* Cambridge: Polity.

Jessop, Bob, and Ngai-Ling Sum. 2001. "Pre-Disciplinary and Post-Disciplinary Perspectives." *New Political Economy* 6(1): 89–101.

Johnson, Chalmers. 2000. *Blowback: The Costs and Consequences of American Empire.* New York: Owl Books.

Jones-Correa, Michael. 1998. *Between Two Nations: The Political Predicament of Latinos in New York City.* Ithaca, N.Y.: Cornell University Press.

Jonsson, P. 2002. "When the Tests Fail." Boston: *Christian Science Monitor* (20 August).

Joshi, S. T. 1999. *Documents of American Prejudice.* New York: Basic Books.

Joshi, S. T., and B. Carter. 1984. "The Role of Labour in the Creation of a Racist Britain." *Race and Class* 25(3): 53–70.

Karenga, Maulana. 1993. *Introduction to Black Studies.* Los Angeles: University of Sankore Press.

Katz, Judy. 1978. *White Awareness: Handbook for Anti-Racism Training.* Norman: University of Oklahoma Press.

Katznelson, Ira. 1976. *Black Men, White Cities.* Chicago: University of Chicago Press.

Kazal, Russell. 1995. "Revisiting Assimilation: The Rise, Fall, and Reappraisal of a Conception in American Ethnic History." *American Historical Review* 100(2): 437–71.

Kelley, Robin. 1997. *Yo' Mama's DisFUNKtional.* Boston: Beacon Press.

King, Anthony D., ed. 1997. *Culture, Globalization, and the World-System: Contemporary Conditions for the Representation of Identity.* Minneapolis: University of Minnesota Press.

Klor de Alva, Jorge, Earl Shorris, and Cornel West. 1996. "Our Next Race Question: The Uneasiness between Blacks and Latinos." *Harper's Magazine* 292(1751) (April): 55–63.

Kohn, Alfie. 1993. *Punished by Rewards.* Boston: Houghton Mifflin.

———. 2000. *The Case against Standardized Testing: Raising Score, Ruining Schools*. Portsmouth, N.H.: Heinemann.

Kotkin, Joel. 1992. *Tribes: How Race, Religion, and Identity Determine Success in the New Global Economy.* New York: Random House.

Kuhl, Stephan. 1994. *The Nazi Connection: Eugenics, American Racism, and German National Socialism*. New York: Oxford University Press.

Kundnani, Arun. 2002. "The Death of Multiculturalism." Institute of Race Relations. (Accessed on-line http://www.irr.org.uk)

Ladson-Billings, Gloria. 1999. "Just What Is Critical Race Theory, and What's It Doing in a Nice Field Like Education?" In Laurence Parker, Donna Deyhle, and Sofia Villenas, eds., *Race Is . . . Race Isn't: Critical Race Theory and Qualitative Studies in Education*. Boulder, Colo.: Westview Press.

Laó-Montes, Agustin, and Arlene Davila. 2000. *Mambo Montage: The Latinization of New York City*. New York: Columbia University Press.

"Lawsuit Charges UPS Discriminates against Its Black Employees." 1997. *Wall Street Journal* (1 May): B6.

Layton-Henry, Zig. 1992. *The Politics of Immigration*. Oxford: Blackwell.

Leadership Education for Asian Pacifics (LEAP). 1993. *Beyond Asian American Poverty: Community Economic Development Policies and Strategies*. Los Angeles: LEAP Asian Pacific American Public Policy Institute.

Lee, Sandra Soo-Jin, Joanne Mountain, and Barbara Koenig. 2001. "The Meaning of 'Race.'" In "The New Genomics: Implications for Health Disparities Research." *Yale Journal of Health Policy, Law, and Ethics* 1: 33–75.

Le-Espiritu, Yen. 1992. *Asian American Panethnicity: Bridging Institutions and Identities*. Philadelphia: Temple University Press.

Lenin, Vladimir Ilyich. 1947. *The Essentials of Lenin*. London: Lawrence and Wishart.

Lerner, Michael, and Cornel West. 1995. *Jews and Blacks: Let the Healing Begin*. New York: G. P. Putnam's Sons.

Lieberman, Leonard. 1968. "The Debate over Race: A Study in the Sociology of Knowledge." *Phylon* 39: 127–41.

———. 2003. "Perishing Paradigm: Race—1930 to 1999." *American Anthropologist* 105 (March).

Littlefield, Alice, Leonard Lieberman, and Larry Reynolds. 1999. "The Debate over Race: Thirty Years and Two Centuries Later; Part Two: Thirty Years after the Debate over Race: The Passing of the Great Consensus." In Ashley Montagu, ed., *Race and I.Q.* New York: Oxford University Press.

Loeb, Paul. 1999. *Soul of a Citizen: Living with Conviction in a Cynical Time*. New York: St. Martin's Press.

López-Garza, Marta, and David R. Diaz. 2001. *Asian and Latino Immigrants in a Restructuring Economy: The Metamorphosis of Southern California*. Palo Alto, Calif.: Stanford University Press.

Lott, Juanita Tamayo. 1993. "Policy Purposes of Race and Ethnicity: An Assessment of Federal Racial and Ethnic Categories." *Ethnicities and Disease* 3 (Summer): 221–28.

Luchsinger, Jose Alejandro. 2001. "Diabetes." In Marilyn Aguirre-Molina, Carlos W. Molina, and Ruth Enid Zambrana, eds., *Health Issues in the Latino Community.* San Francisco: Jossey Bass.

Lugo, Alejandro. 2004. *Fragmented Lives, Assembled Parts: Culture, Capitalism, and Conquest at the U.S.-Mexico Border.* Austin: University of Texas Press.

Macedo, Donaldo, Bessie Dendrinos, and Panayota Gounari. 2003. *The Hegemony of English.* Boulder, Colo.: Paradigm Press.

Maciel, David R., and María Herrera-Sobek, eds. 1998. *Culture across Borders: Mexican Immigration and Popular Culture.* Tucson: University of Arizona Press.

Maldonado-Denis, Manuel. 1972. *Puerto Rico: A Socio-Historic Interpretation.* New York: Random House.

Malik, Kenan. 1996. *The Meaning of Race: Race, History, and Culture in Western Society.* New York: New York University Press.

Marable, Manning. 1995. *Beyond Black and White: Transforming African American Politics.* London: Verso.

———. 1998. "Being Left: A Humane Society Is Possible through Struggle." *Z Magazine* interview with Manning Marable. (Accessed on-line at www.znet.org)

———. 2000. "We Need a New and Critical Study of Race and Ethnicity." *Chronicle of Higher Education* 46(i): 25, B4.

Mariscal, Jorge. 2003. "A Chicano Looks at the Trent Lott Affair." *Black Commentator* 25 (January 16): 1. (Accessed on-line at http://www.blackcommentator.com/25/25_guest_commentary.html)

Martino, Wayne, and Bob Meyenn, eds. 2001. *What about the Boys? Issues of Masculinity in Schools.* Buckingham, U.K.: Open University Press.

Matiki, Alfred J. 2001. "The Social Significance of English in Malawi." *World Englishes* 20(2) (July).

Matsuda, Mari, Charles Lawrence, Richard Delgado, and Kimberlé Crenshaw. 1993. *Words That Wound: Critical Race Theory, Assaultive Speech, and the First Amendment.* Boulder, Colo.: Westview Press.

Marx, Anthony W. 1998. *Making Race and Nation: A Comparison of South Africa, the United States, and Brazil.* Cambridge: Cambridge University Press.

Marx, Karl, and Frederick Engels. 1970. *The German Ideology.* New York: International Publishers.

McChesney, Robert W. 2001. "Global Media, Neoliberalism, and Imperialism." *Monthly Review* 49(9) (February): 1–13.

McLemee, Scott. 1996. *C. L. R. James on the "Negro Question."* Jackson: University Press of Mississippi.

McNally, David. 1997. "Language, History, and Class Struggle." In Ellen Meiksins Wood and John Bellamy Foster, eds., *In Defense of History: Marxism and the Postmodern Agenda.* New York: Monthly Review Press.

McNeil, Linda. 1986. *The Contradictions of Control: School Structure and School Knowledge.* New York and London: Routledge.

———. 2000. *Contradictions of School Reform: Educational Costs of Standardized Testing.* New York: Routledge.

McNeil, Linda, and Angela Valenzuela. 2000. "The Harmful Impact of the TAAS System of Testing in Texas: Beneath the Accountability Rhetoric." Cambridge, Mass.: Harvard University Civil Rights Project. (Available at www.law.harvard.edu/groups/civilrights/testing.htm)

Meiksins, Peter. 1998. "Confronting the Time Bind: Work, Family, and Capitalism." *Monthly Review* 49(9) (February): 1–19.

Memmi, Albert. 2000. *Racism.* Minneapolis: University of Minnesota Press.

Merl, Jean. 1997. "City Still Viewed as Racially Split." *Los Angeles Times* (29 April).

Michael, John. 2000. *Anxious Intellects.* Durham, N.C.: Duke University Press.

Miles, Robert. 1982. *Racism and Migrant Labor.* New York: Routledge and Kegan Paul.

———. 1984. "Marxism versus the Sociology of Race Relations." *Ethnic and Racial Studies* 7(2) (April): 217–37.

———. 1989. *Racism.* Key Ideas series. London: Routledge.

———. 1993. *Racism after "Race Relations."* London: Routledge.

Miles, Robert, and Malcolm Brown. 2003. *Racism* (2d ed.). London: Routledge.

Miles, Robert, and A. Phizacklea. 1981. "Racism and Capitalist Decline." In Michael Harloe, ed., *New Perspectives in Urban Change and Conflict,* 80–l00. London: Heinemann Educational Books.

Miles, Robert, and Rodolfo D. Torres. 1999. "Does 'Race' Matter? Transatlantic Perspectives on Racism after 'Race Relations.'" In Rodolfo D. Torres, Louis F. Mirón, and Jonathan X. Inda, eds., *Race, Identity, and Citizenship.* Oxford: Blackwell.

Miliband, Ralph. 1969. *The State in Capitalist Society.* New York: Basic Books.

———. 1989. *Divided Societies: Class Struggle in Contemporary Capitalism.* Oxford: Oxford University Press.

Mills, Charles. 1997. *The Racial Contract.* Ithaca, N.Y.: Cornell University Press.

Mills, C. Wright. 2002. *The Sociological Imagination.* London: Oxford University Press.

Mirandé, Alfredo. 1997. *Hombres y Machos: Masculinity and Latino Culture.* Boulder, Colo.: Westview Press.

Mirón, Louis, and Jonathan X. Inda. 2004. "Transnational Urbanism, Transcitizenship, and the Implications for the New World Order." In Cameron McCarthy and Warren Krichlow, eds. *Race, Identity, and Representation in Education* (2d ed.). New York: Routledge.

Mishel, Lawrence, Jared Bernstein, and Heather Boushey. 2003. *The State of Working America, 2002/2003.* Ithaca, N.Y.: Cornell University Press.

Molnar, Alex. 1996. *Giving Kids the Business: The Commercialization of American Schools.* Boulder, Colo.: Westview Press.

Montagu, Ashley. 1972. *Statement on Race.* London: Oxford University Press.

———. 1974. *Man's Most Dangerous Myth: The Fallacy of Race* (rev. ed.). New York: Oxford University Press.

Montejano, David. 1987. *Anglos and Mexicans in the Making of Texas, 1836–1986.* Austin: University of Texas Press.

Morrison, Toni. 1989. "Unspeakable Things Unspoken: The Afro-American Presence in American Literature." *Michigan Quarterly Review* 28 (Winter).

Moure-Eraso, R., and G. Friedman-Jiménez. 2001. "Occupational Health among Latino Workers in Urban Settings." In Marilyn Aguirre-Molina, Carlos W. Molina, and Ruth Enid Zambrana, eds., *Health Issues in the Latino Community.* San Francisco: Jossey Bass.

Muñoz, Carlos. 1989. *Youth, Identity, Power: The Chicano Movement.* London: Verso.

Naiman, Joanne. 1996. "Left Feminism and the Return to Class." *Monthly Review* 48(2) (June): 12–28.

National Council of La Raza. 2003. "Administration Misuses Criminal Database, Unlawfully Targets Immigrants." December 17. (Available at http://www.nclr.policy.net)

NCES (National Center for Education Statistics). 2001. *Dropout Rates in the United States.* Washington, D.C.: U.S. Department of Education.

Nettle, Daniel, and Suzanne Romaine. 2000. *Vanishing Voices: The Extinction of the World's Languages.* New York: Oxford University Press.

Ngin, ChorSwang. 1995. "Racialized Struggles in Suburbia: Contested Ideologies on Belonging." *California Politics and Policy* 1: 75–84.

———. 1996. "Racism and Racialized Discourse on the Asian Youth." *California Politics and Policy* 2: 83–102.

Nieto, Sonia. 1996. *Affirming Diversity* (2d ed.). New York: Longman Publishers.

Noriega, Chon. 1993. "El Hilo Latino: Representation, Identity, and National Culture." *Jump Cut* 38: 45–50.

Oboler, Suzanne. 1995. *Ethnic Labels, Latino Lives: Identity and the Politics of (Re)Presentation in the United States.* Minneapolis: University of Minnesota Press.

Omi, Michael. 1993. "Out of the Melting Pot and into the Fire." In *The State of Asian Pacific America: Policy Issues to the Year 2000*, 199–214. Los Angeles: LEAP Asian Pacific American Public Policy Institute and UCLA Asian American Studies Center.

Omi, Michael, and Howard Winant. 1986. *Racial Formation in the United States: From the 1960s to the 1980s*. New York: Routledge.

———. 1993. "On the Theoretical Status of the Concept of Race." In Cameron McCarthy and Warren Crichlow, eds., *Race, Identity, and Representation*. New York: Routledge.

———. 1994. *Racial Formation in the United States: From the 1960s to the 1990s* (2d ed.). New York: Routledge.

Ong, Aiwah. 2003. *Buddha Is Hiding: Refugees, Citizenship, and the New America*. Berkeley: University of California Press.

Ong, Aiwah, and Don Nonini, eds. 1997. *Ungrounded Empires: The Cultural Politics of Modern Chinese Transnationalism*. New York: Routledge.

Ong, Paul, ed. 2000. *Transforming Race Relations: A Public Policy Report*. Los Angeles: LEAP Asian Pacific American Public Policy Institute and UCLA Asian American Studies Center.

Ong, Paul, and Evelyn Blumenberg. 1997. "Scientists and Engineers." In Darrell Hamamoto and Rodolfo D. Torres, eds., *New American Destinies: A Reader in Contemporary Asian and Latino Immigration*, 163–81. New York: Routledge.

Padilla, Felix M. 1985. *Latino Ethnic Consciousness: The Case of Mexican Americans and Puerto Ricans in Chicago*. Notre Dame, Ind.: University of Notre Dame Press.

Pan, Lynn. 1990. *Sons of the Yellow Emperor: A History of the Chinese Diaspora*. New York: Kodansha International.

Pardo, Mary. 1998. *Mexican American Women Activists: Identity and Resistance in Two Los Angeles Communities*. Philadelphia: Temple University Press.

Parenti, Michael. 1995. *Against Empire*. San Francisco: City Lights Books.

Patterson, Sheila. 1963. *Dark Strangers*. London: Tavislock Publications.

Perez-Stable, E., T. Juarbe, and G. Moreno-John. 2001. "Cardiovascular Disease." In Marilyn Aguirre-Molina, Carlos W. Molina, and Ruth Enid Zambrana, eds., *Health Issues in the Latino Community*. San Francisco: Jossey Bass.

Piven, Frances Fox, and Richard Cloward. 1998. "Eras of Power." *Monthly Review* 49(8) (January): 11–23.

Poblete, Juan. 2003. *Critical Latin American and Latino Studies*. Minneapolis: University of Minnesota Press.

Popham, James. 1999. "Why Standardized Tests Don't Measure Educational Quality." *Educational Leadership* (March): 8–15.

Postal, Danny. 2002. "Is Race Real? How Does Identity Matter?" *Chronicle of Higher Education* (April 5): A10.

Poulantzas, Nicos. 1973. *Political Power and Social Classes*. London: New Left Books.

Powers, Samantha. 2002. *"A Problem from Hell": America and the Age of Genocide*. New York: Perennial.

Quijano, Anibal. 2000. "Coloniality of Power, Ethnocentrism, and Latin America." *Nepantla* 1(3): 533–80.

Ramirez, A. G., and L. Suarez. 2001. "The Impact of Cancer on Latino Populations." In Marilyn Aguirre-Molina, Carlos W. Molina, and Ruth Enid Zambrana, eds., *Health Issues in the Latino Community*. San Francisco: Jossey Bass.

Reed, Adolph, Jr. 1998. "Skin Deep." *Village Voice* (24 September): 2.

Rex, John. 1970. *Race Relations in Sociological Theory*. London: Weidenfeld and Nicolson.

Reynolds, Larry T. 1992. "A Retrospective on 'Race': The Career of a Concept." *Sociological Focus* 25(1): 1–14.

Richmond, Anthony. 1955. *The Colour Problem*. New York: Penguin Books.

Rodriguez, Clara. 2000. *Changing Race: Latinos, the Census, and the History of Ethnicity in the United States*. New York: New York University Press.

Rodriguez, Gregory. 1996. *The Emerging Latino Middle Class*. Malibu, Calif.: Institute for Public Policy, Pepperdine University.

Rodríguez, Juana María. 2003. *Queer Latinidad: Identity, Practices, Discursive Spaces*. New York: New York University Press.

Roediger, David R. 1994. *Towards the Abolition of Whiteness: Essays on Race, Politics, and Working Class History*. London: Verso.

———. 1998. *Black on White: Black Writers on What It Means to Be White*. New York: Schocken Books.

Roithmayr, Daria. 1999. "Introduction to Critical Race Theory." In Laurence Parker, Donna Deyhle, and Sofia Villenas, eds., *Race Is . . . Race Isn't: Critical Race Theory and Qualitative Studies in Education*. Boulder, Colo.: Westview Press.

Román, David, and Albert Sandoval. 1995. "Caught in the Web: Latinidad, AIDS, and Allegory in *Kiss of the Spider Woman*, the Musical." *American Literature* 67(3) (September): 580–98.

Rosaldo, Renato. 1989. *Culture and Truth: The Remaking of Social Analysis*. Boston: Beacon Press.

———. 1994. "Social Justice and the Crisis of National Communities." *Cultural Anthropology* 9(3): 402–11.

Rowan, Leslie, Michelle Knobel, Chris Bigum, and Colin Lankshear. 2002. *Boys, Literacies, and Schooling: The Dangerous Territories of Gender-Based Literacy Reform*. Buckingham, U.K.: Open University Press.

Rowan, T. Carl. 1996. *The Coming Race War in America: A Wake-Up Call.* Boston: Little, Brown.

Roy, Arundhati. 2003. "Instant-Mix Imperial Democracy (Buy One, Get One Free)." Presented at the Center for Economic and Social Rights, at the Riverside Church, New York (May 13). (Available at http://www.cesr.org/roy/images/roy.pdf)

Ryan, R., and J. G. La Guardia. 1999. "Achievement Motivation within a Pressured Society: Intrinsic and Extrinsic Motivations to Learn and the Politics of School Reform." In *Advances in Motivation and Achievement*, vol. 11. Stamford, Conn.: JAI Press.

Sacks. Peter. 1999. *Standardized Minds: The High Price of America's Testing Culture and What We Can Do to Change It.* Cambridge, Mass.: Perseus.

Saldivar-Hull, Sonia. 2000. *Feminism on the Border: Chicana Gender Politics and Literature.* Berkeley: University of California Press.

Santa Ana, Otto. 2002. *Brown Tide Rising: Metaphors of Latinos in Contemporary American Public Discourse.* Austin: University of Texas Press.

Sassen, Saskia. 1996. "New Employment Regimes in Cities: The Impact on Immigrant Workers." *New Community* 22: 579–94.

———. 1998. *Globalization and Its Discontents.* New York: New Press.

———. 2001. *The Global City.* Princeton, N.J.: Princeton University Press.

Sayer, Andrew. 1999. "Long Live Postdisciplinary Studies! Sociology and the Curse of Disciplinary Parochialism/Imperialism." Paper presented to the British Sociological Association Conference, Glasgow, UK (April). Published by the Department of Sociology, Lancaster University. (Available at http://www.comp.lancs.ac.uk/sociology/soc025as.html)

Scott, Allen, and Edward Soja. 1996. *The City: Los Angeles and Urban Theory and the End of the Twentieth Century.* Berkeley: University of California Press.

Skelton, Christine. 2001. *Schooling the Boys: Masculinities and Primary Education.* Buckingham, U.K.: Open University Press.

Skutnabb-Kangas, Tove. 2000. *Linguistic Genocide in Education—or Worldwide Diversity and Human Rights?* Mahwah, N.J.: Lawrence Erlbaum.

Small, Stephen. 1994. *Racialised Barriers: The Black Experience in the United States and England in the 1980s.* London: Routledge.

———. 1999. "The Contours of Racialization: Structures, Representations, and Resistance in the United States." In Rodolfo D. Torres, Louis F. Miron, and Jonathan X. Inda, eds., *Race, Identity, and Citizenship.* Oxford: Blackwell.

Smith, Susan J. 1989. *The Politics of "Race" and Residence.* Cambridge: Polity.

Solomos, John. 1989. *Race and Racism in Contemporary Britain.* London: Macmillan.

Solórzano, Daniel G. 1998. "Critical Race Theory, Race and Microaggresssions, and the Experience of Chicana and Chicano Scholars." *International Journal of Qualitative Studies in Education* 11: 121–36.

Sowell, Thomas. 1994. *Race and Culture: A World View.* New York: Basic Books.

Steinberg, Stephen. 1995. *Turning Back: The Retreat from Racial Justice in American Thought and Policy.* Boston: Beacon Press.

Suro, Roberto, 1999. *Strangers among Us: Latino Lives in a Changing America.* New York: Vintage Books.

Sweezy, Paul, and Harry Magdoff. 2001. "The New Economy: Myth and Reality." *Monthly Review* 52(1) (April): 1–15.

Tabb, William. 1997. "Conceptualizing Globalization." *Monthly Review* 49(6) (November): 35–39.

Taguieff, Pierre-André. 2001. *The Force of Prejudice: On Racism and Its Doubles.* Minneapolis: University of Minnesota Press.

Takaki, Ronald. 1989. *Strangers from a Different Shore.* Boston: Little, Brown.

Tate, William F. 1997. "Critical Race Theory and Education: History, Theory, and Implications." In Michael Apple, ed., *Review of Research in Education,* no. 22: 195–250. Washington D.C.: American Educational Research Association.

Thernstrom, Abigail, and Stephan Thernstrom. 2003. *No Excuses: Closing the Racial Gap in Learning.* New York: Simon and Schuster.

Toch, Thomas. 1991. *In the Name of Excellence.* New York: Oxford University Press.

Tololyan, Khachig. 1995. "A Note from the Editor." *Diaspora* 4(1) (Spring): 1.

Tornatzky, Louis, Elsa Macias, and Sara Jones. 2002. *Latinos and Information Technology: The Promise and the Challenge.* Claremont, Calif.: Tomás Rivera Policy Institute (February).

Torres, Andrés, and José E. Velázquez. 1998. *The Puerto Rican Movement: Voices from the Diaspora.* Philadelphia: Temple University Press.

Torres, Rodolfo D., and George Katsiaficas. 1999. *Latino Social Movements: Historical and Theoretical Perspectives.* New York and London: Routledge.

Torres, Rodolfo D., and ChorSwang Ngin. 1995. "Racialized Boundaries, Class Relations, and Cultural Politics: The Asian-American and Latino Experience." In Antonia Darder, ed., *Culture and Difference: Critical Perspective on the Bicultural Experience in the United States,* 55–69. Westport, Conn.: Bergin and Garvey.

Torres-Saillant, Silvio. 2003. "Inventing the Race: Latinos and the Ethnoracial Pentagon." *Latinos Studies* 1(1) (March): 123–51.

Torres-Saillant, Silvio, and Ramona Hernandez. 1998. *The Dominican Americans.* Westport, Conn.: Greenwood Publishing.

Truong, Thann-dam. 1990. *Sex, Money, and Morality: Prostitution and Tourism in Southeast Asia.* Atlantic Highlands, N.J.: Zed Books.

U.S. Bureau of Labor Statistics. 2001. Table 4: "Fatal Occupational Injuries and Employment by Selected Worker Characteristics, 2000." (Accessed on-line at www.bls.gov/news.release/cfoi.t04.htm, 27 May 2001)

U.S. Census Bureau. 2001a. *Profile of General Demographic Characteristics: 2000.* Washington, D.C.: U.S. Department of Commerce.

U.S. Census Bureau. 2001b. Table 11: "Major Occupation Group of the Employed Civilian Population 16 Years and Over by Sex, and Race and Hispanic Origin: March 2000." Washington, D.C.: U.S. Department of Commerce.

U.S. Census Bureau. 2001c. Table 7: "Educational Attainment of the Population 25 Years and Over by Sex, and Race and Hispanic Origin: March 2000." Washington, D.C.: U.S. Department of Commerce.

Valle, Victor, and Rodolfo D. Torres. 1994. "Latinos in a 'Post-Industrial' Disorder: Politics in a Changing City." *Socialist Review* 23(4): 1–28.

———. 1995. "The Idea of Mestizaje and the 'Race' Problematic: Racialized Media Discourse in a Post-Fordist Landscape." In Antonia Darder, ed., *Culture and Difference: Critical Perspectives on the Bicultural Experience in the United States.* Westport, Conn.: Bergin and Garvey.

———. 1998. "Latinos in a 'Post-industrial' Disorder: Politics in a Changing City." In Antonia Darder and Rodolfo Torres, eds., *The Latino Studies Reader: Culture, Economy, and Society.* Oxford: Blackwell.

———. 2000. *Latino Metropolis.* Minneapolis: University of Minnesota Press.

Van den Berghe, Pierre L. 1978. *Race and Racism: A Comparative Perspective.* New York: John Wiley.

van Dijk, T. A. 1993. *Elite Discourses on Racism.* Newbury Park, Calif.: Sage.

Vázquez, Francisco H., and Rodolfo D. Torres, eds. 2003. *Latino/a Thought: Culture, Politics, and Society.* Lanham, Md.: Rowman and Littlefield.

Vélez-Ibáñez, Carlos G. 1996. *Border Visions: Mexican Cultures of the Southwest United States.* Tucson: University of Arizona Press.

Viadero, Debra. 1999. "Standford Report Questions Accuracy of Tests." *Education Week* (6 October): 3.

Villenas, Sofia, Donna Deyhle, and Laurence Parker. 1999. "Critical Race Theory and Praxis: Chicano(a)/Latino(a) and Navajo Struggles for Dignity, Educational Equity, and Social Justice." In Laurence Parker, Donna Deyhle, and Sofia Villenas, eds., *Race Is . . . Race Isn't: Critical Race Theory and Qualitative Studies in Education.* Boulder, Colo.: Westview Press.

Viotti da Costa, Emilia. 2001. "New Publics, New Politics, New Histories: From Economic Reductionism to Cultural Reductionism—In Search of Dialectics." In Gilbert M. Joseph, ed., *Reclaiming the Political in Latin American History: Essays from the North.* Durham, N.C.: Duke University Press.

Wainwright, Hilary. 2003. *Reclaim the State: Experiments in Popular Democracy.* London: Verso.

Ward, Kathryn. 1990. *Women Workers and Global Restructuring*. New York: Cornell University School of Industrial and Labor Relations.

Watts, Steven. 1991. "The Idiocy of American Studies: Poststructuralism, Language, and Politics in the Age of Self-Fulfillment." *American Quarterly* 43(4) (December): 625–60.

Wellman, David T. 1993. *Portraits of White Racism* (2d ed.). Cambridge: Cambridge University Press.

West, Cornel. 1993. *Race Matters*. Boston: Beacon Press.

———. 1994. *Race Matters*. New York: Vintage Books.

White, E. Frances. 1990. "Africa on My Mind: Gender, Counter Discourse, and African American Nationalism." *Journal of Women's History* 2(1) (Spring): 73–97.

Wieviorka, Michek. 1997. "Is It Difficult to Be an Anti-Racist?" In Pnina Werbner and Tariq Modood, eds., *Debating Cultural Hybridity: Multi-Cultural Identities and the Politics of Anti-Racism*. Atlantic Highlands, N.J.: Zed Books.

William, Fiona. 1989. *Social Policy: A Critical Introduction*. Cambridge: Polity.

Williams, David R. 1994. "The Concept of Race in Health Services Research: 1966 to 1990." *Health Services Research* 29: 261.

Williamson, Thad, David Imbroscio, and Gar Alperovitz. 2002. *Making a Place for Community: Local Democracy in a Global Era*. New York: Routledge.

Wilson, William J. 1980. *The Declining Significance of Race: Blacks and Changing American Institutions* (2d ed.). Chicago: University of Chicago Press.

———. 1987/1990. *The Truly Disadvantaged*. Chicago: University of Chicago Press.

———. 1997. *When Work Disappears: The World of the New Urban Poor*. New York: Vintage.

———. 1999. *The Bridge over the Racial Divide: Rising Inequality and Coalition Politics*. Berkeley: University of California Press.

Winant, Howard. 1994. *Racial Conditions: Politics, Theory, Comparisons*. Minneapolis: University of Minnesota Press.

———. 2000. "Back to the Future." *Race and Society* 2(2): 217–20.

Wing, Adrien Katherine. 1997. *Critical Race Feminism: A Reader*. New York: New York University Press.

———. 2003. *Critical Race Feminism: A Reader* (2d ed.). New York: New York University Press.

Wong, Sau-Ling. 1995. "Denationalization Reconsidered: Asian American Cultural Criticism at a Theoretical Crossroads." *Amerasia Journal* 21(1–2): 1–27.

Wood, Ellen M. 1994. "Identity Crisis." *In These Times* (June): 28–29.

———. 1995. *Democracy against Capitalism: Renewing Historical Materialism*. New York: Cambridge University Press.

———. 1996. "Modernity, Postmodernity, or Capitalism." *Monthly Review* 48(3): 21–39.

———. 1998. "Modernity, Postmodernity, or Capitalism?" In Robert N. McChesney, Ellen Meiksins Wood, and John Bellamy Foster, eds., *Capitalism and the Information Age*. New York: Monthly Review Press.

———. 2003. *Empire of Capital*. New York and London: Verso.

Wood, Michael. 2002. *Conquistadors*. Berkeley: University of California Press.

Woodward, Will, ed. 2003. "Culture of Tests 'Stifling' Joy of Learning." *Guardian*, U.K. (17 April). (Accessed on-line at http://www.EducationGuardian.co.uk)

Wright, Erik Olin. 1997. *Class Counts: Comparative Studies in Class Analysis*. New York: Cambridge University Press.

Zavala, Iris. 1992. *Colonialism and Culture: Hispanic Modernism and the Social Imaginary*. Bloomington and Indianapolis: Indiana University Press.

Index

About the Authors

Antonia Darder is Professor of Educational Policy Studies and Latina/Latino Studies at the University of Illinois at Urbana-Champaign. Her publications include *Culture and Power in the Classroom, Reinventing Paulo Freire,* and *The Latino Studies Reader: Culture, Economy, and Society.*

Rodolfo D. Torres is Associate Professor of Chicano-Latino Studies, Political Science, and Planning, Policy, and Design at the University of California, Irvine and is a member of the Focused Research Program in Labor Studies at the University of California, Irvine. His books include *Latino Metropolis, Latino Social Movements,* and *Latino/a Thought.*